IXL MATH WORKBOOK

THE ULTIMATE
FOURTH GRADE
MATH WORKBOOK

ISBN: 9781947569515
27 26 25 24 23 9 10 11 12 13

Printed in the USA

Let's Learn!

Numbers are made up of digits. The **value** of each digit depends on its **place**. You can use a place value chart to find the place and value of each digit. For example, look at the chart for 4,193,592 below.

Millions		Hundred thousands	Ten thousands	Thousands		Hundreds	Tens	Ones
4	,	1	9	3	,	5	9	2

Write the place of each highlighted digit.

5 , **7** 8 2

_____HUNDREDS_____

41 , 8 **0** 3

_____

8 7 , 4 0 1

_____

1 6 **7** , 4 9 4

_____

5 , 4 9 3 , 1 6 **2**

_____

7 , **9** 0 0 , 4 2 5

_____

IXL.com skill ID

Y7Q

For more practice, visit IXL.com or the IXL mobile app and enter this code in the search bar.

Place value

Write the value of each highlighted **digit.**

6,5**7**4

_____70_____

9,960

_____

3,61**8**

_____

32,516

_____

42,685

_____

91,**3**63

_____

100,8**2**1

_____

12**1**,482

_____

112,618

_____

4,265,799

_____

7,**1**00,808

_____

2,293,456

_____

6,607,**7**06

_____

3,134,5**8**2

_____

5,**5**00,500

_____

IXL.com
skill ID
WLP

Write each number. Then answer each question.

Write a 4-digit number that has a 9 in the tens place, a 5 in the thousands place, and a 2 in the other places.

_5,292_

What is the value of the digit in the hundreds place?

_200_

Write a 5-digit number that has a 4 in the tens place, a 3 in the ten-thousands place, a 5 in the thousands place, and a 1 in the other places.

_____

What is the value of the digit in the ten-thousands place?

_____

Write a 6-digit number that has a 5 in the ones place, a 7 in the hundred-thousands place, a 4 in the thousands place, and a 0 in all of the other places.

_____

What is the value of the digit in the thousands place?

_____

IXL.com
skill ID
B5N

Let's Learn!

To write a number in **expanded form**, write it as the sum of the value of each digit. See the example below.

$$45,698 = 40,000 + 5,000 + 600 + 90 + 8$$

Write each number in expanded form.

5,407 = _____ 5,000 + 400 + 7 _____

17,843 = _____

48,004 = _____

201,065 = _____

Write each number.

4,000 + 200 + 70 + 5 = _____ 4,275 _____

200,000 + 80,000 + 3,000 + 500 + 80 + 1 = _____

50,000 + 6,000 + 80 + 3 = _____

600,000 + 2,000 + 300 + 90 = _____

IXL.com
skill ID
M5V

Write each number.

one hundred seventy-six thousand nine hundred   _176,900_

sixty-one thousand seven hundred one   _____

four hundred twenty-five thousand   _____

nine hundred thousand   _____

three hundred thousand six hundred   _____

Write each number in word form.

20,580   TWENTY THOUSAND FIVE HUNDRED EIGHTY

648,000   _____

91,200   _____

700,030   _____

IXL.com
skill ID
5G4

Draw lines to match the two forms of the same number.

20,000 + 7,000 + 50   500,000 + 80,000 + 5,000 + 400

300,710   207,050

5,000 + 800 + 50 + 4   300,000 + 700 + 10

275,000   twenty-seven thousand fifty

585,400   37,100

three thousand   two hundred seventy-five
seventeen   thousand

200,000 + 7,000 + 50   3,000 + 10 + 7

thirty-seven thousand   five thousand
one hundred   eight hundred fifty-four

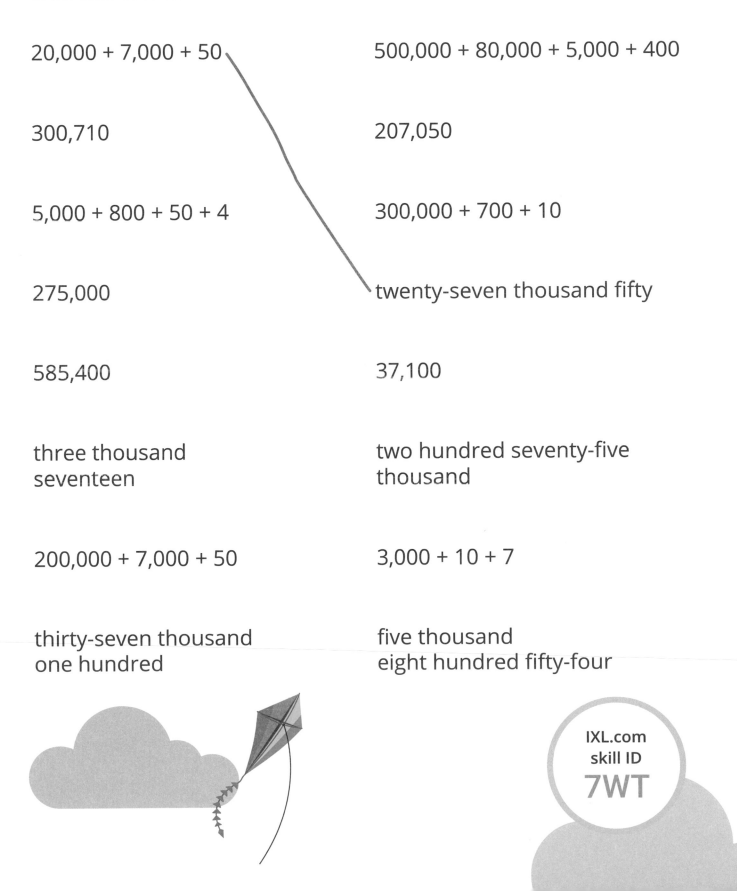

Let's Learn!

You can represent numbers in different ways. For example, 200 can be represented as 2 hundreds or 20 tens.

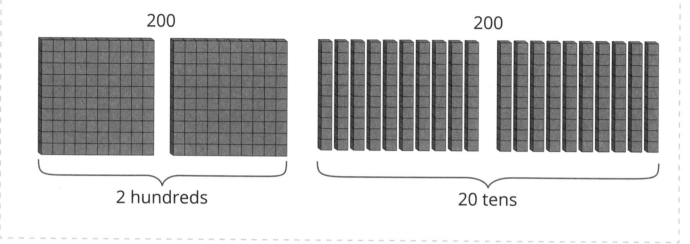

Write the number that makes the statement true.

1,200 = ___12___ hundreds

50 tens = _____

_____ hundreds = 3,600

_____ tens = 780

42 hundreds = _____

920 = _____ tens

_____ = 89 tens

63 tens = _____

300 = _____ tens

72 hundreds = _____

Write the number that makes the statement true.

37 hundreds = _____

_____ tens = 540

_____ hundreds = 2,400

83 tens = _____

68 tens = _____

_____ hundreds = 7,400

_____ hundreds = 9,100

26 tens = _____

95 tens = _____

_____ hundreds = 3,200

_____ tens = 700

95 hundreds = _____

Let's Learn!

You can use a place value chart to compare numbers. Let's try it with 792,130 and 758,342. Compare each digit from left to right.

Hundred thousands	Ten thousands	Thousands		Hundreds	Tens	Ones
7	9	2	,	1	3	0
7	5	8	,	3	4	2

First, compare the digits in the hundred-thousands place. Those digits are the same, so move to the ten-thousands place. You know that 90,000 is greater than 50,000, so 792,130 > 758,342.

Compare each pair of numbers. Fill in each circle with >, <, or =.

14,573 ◯ 18,009   10,300 ◯ 7,890

16,421 ◯ 16,391   45,912 ◯ 44,879

52,581 ◯ 52,581   60,120 ◯ 59,938

79,402 ◯ 79,412   97,241 ◯ 100,325

Compare each pair of numbers. Fill in each circle with >, <, or =.

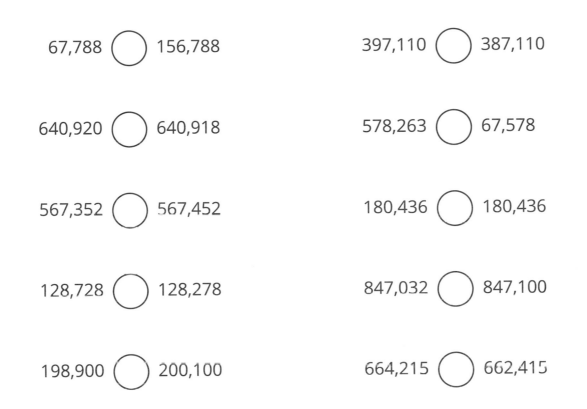

67,788 ◯ 156,788   397,110 ◯ 387,110

640,920 ◯ 640,918   578,263 ◯ 67,578

567,352 ◯ 567,452   180,436 ◯ 180,436

128,728 ◯ 128,278   847,032 ◯ 847,100

198,900 ◯ 200,100   664,215 ◯ 662,415

Write a number that makes the statement true.

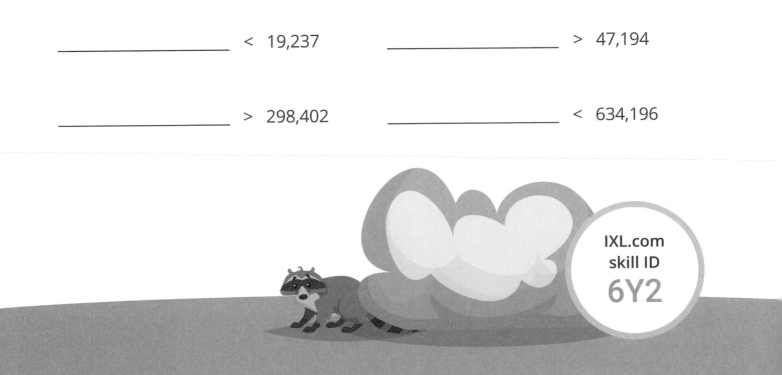

_____ < 19,237   _____ > 47,194

_____ > 298,402   _____ < 634,196

Write the numbers in order from least to greatest.

12,521 7,892 10,985 _____ _____ _____

98,354 100,002 98,954 _____ _____ _____

120,723 102,964 102,825 _____ _____ _____

641,306 642,050 641,297 _____ _____ _____

854,458 854,500 854,462 _____ _____ _____

1,000,000 993,150 987,002 _____ _____ _____

Answer each question.

In October, a cell phone company made $996,325. In November, it made $992,080. In which month did the cell phone company make more money?

_____

Corrin wants to hike three mountains over her summer break. She will hike the mountains in order from shortest to tallest.

Mountain	Mount Sheila	Flat Peak	Ranger Mountain
Height	13,171 feet	13,810 feet	13,534 feet

Which mountain will she hike last?

_____

A hip-hop group performed in four different cities.

City	Seattle	Chicago	Houston	Baltimore
Tickets sold	34,758	38,587	34,700	38,489

In which city were the most tickets sold?

_____

In which city were the fewest tickets sold?

_____

Let's Learn!

You can round numbers to any place value. Look at the digit that is one place to the right of the place you are rounding to. If that digit is 5 or greater, round up. Try it with 2,379.

2,379   To round to the nearest **hundred**, look at the **tens** place.

There is a 7 in the tens place. Since 7 is greater than 5, the 3 in the hundreds place rounds up to 4.

2,400   So, 2,379 rounded to the nearest hundred is 2,400.

2,379   To round to the nearest **thousand**, look at the **hundreds** place.

There is a 3 in the hundreds place. Since 3 is less than 5, the 2 in the thousands place does not round up.

2,000   So, 2,379 rounded to the nearest thousand is 2,000.

Round each number to the nearest hundred.

728   _____700_____   245   _____

5,792   _____   3,867   _____

34,633   _____   98,581   _____

126,374 _____   425,103 _____

542,316 _____   607,452 _____

Round each number to the nearest thousand.

6,943   __7,000__   9,526   _____

18,329   _____   27,840   _____

384,474   _____   405,287   _____

618,732   _____   933,095   _____

Round each number to the nearest ten thousand.

43,642   __40,000__   91,782   _____

68,019   _____   205,799   _____

594,900   _____   837,003   _____

1,176,354   _____

IXL.com
skill ID
QV7

CHALLENGE ZONE

Circle the number that matches all of the clues.

I am greater than 42,000.

If you round me to the nearest ten thousand, you will get 40,000.

There is an even digit in my tens place.

46,351	42,230	40,984
41,101	39,263	45,213
43,243	46,149	47,324

If you round me to the nearest hundred thousand, you will get 300,000.

I am less than 287,000.

The digit in my hundreds place is the same as the digit in my thousands place.

361,139	286,605	286,451
288,873	289,456	317,723
339,145	247,754	322,827

If you round me to the nearest ten thousand, you will get 650,000.

I am greater than 652,172.

If you round me to the nearest thousand, you will **not** get 653,000.

650,902	651,237	653,481
643,297	652,045	645,236
648,229	655,037	654,181

You can round to *estimate* the answer to a problem. Try it yourself! Estimate by rounding the numbers to the nearest ten thousand.

14,037 + 77,107 is about ___10,000___ + ___80,000___ = ___90,000___

63,489 − 28,273 is about _____ − _____ = _____

23,683 + 48,293 is about _____ + _____ = _____

79,583 − 31,309 is about _____ − _____ = _____

Estimate by rounding the numbers to the nearest hundred thousand.

168,702 + 291,560 is about ___200,000___ + ___300,000___ = ___500,000___

842,831 − 421,913 is about _____ − _____ = _____

322,794 + 382,310 is about _____ + _____ = _____

783,010 − 209,011 is about _____ − _____ = _____

Let's Learn!

You can use the following steps to add. Look at the example. Remember to regroup.

```
  2 4 , 3 6 3        1              1
+ 5 7 , 3 7 4     2 4 , 3 6 3    2 4 , 3 6 3
───────────     + 5 7 , 3 7 4   + 5 7 , 3 7 4
          7     ───────────     ───────────
                        3 7           7 3 7
```

```
   1     1         1      1
  2 4 , 3 6 3     2 4 , 3 6 3
+ 5 7 , 3 7 4   + 5 7 , 3 7 4
───────────     ───────────
    1 , 7 3 7     8 1 , 7 3 7
```

So, 24,363 + 57,374 = 81,737!

Add.

```
  5 3 , 7 7 4        7 6 , 3 8 5        4 3 , 4 8 0
+ 4 2 , 4 1 7      + 3 2 , 9 1 4      + 3 8 , 2 3 9
───────────        ───────────        ───────────
```

```
  2 4 , 3 8 6        1 3 , 4 1 6        5 9 , 8 2 7
+ 7 1 , 8 7 3      + 8 5 , 9 5 9      + 3 7 , 1 6 8
───────────        ───────────        ───────────
```

Add.

```
   17,342          39,660          37,726
 +47,577        +31,588        +25,945
```

```
   49,737          19,379          63,048
 +28,476        +80,184        +28,986
```

```
  422,685         354,984         865,908
+121,482       +101,618       +125,915
```

```
  136,199         720,856         269,859
+561,774       +265,309       +615,644
```

Add. Find the row, column, or diagonal where all of the answers have the same digit in the **thousands place**.

595,289 +213,716	46,204 +82,527	434,712 +264,524
53,532 +74,894	26,528 +52,613	436,467 +171,889
257,823 +731,341	472,724 +466,426	24,485 +84,214

Add.

```
  1  11
  2,827
  1,281
+ 2,472
─────────
  6,580
```

```
  5,344
  3,853
+ 4,081
─────────
```

```
  36,832
  37,903
+ 52,492
──────────
```

```
  59,238
  17,442
+ 65,902
──────────
```

```
  83,398
  74,550
+ 26,492
──────────
```

```
  92,244
  53,760
+ 88,238
──────────
```

```
  272,504
  404,395
+ 180,478
───────────
```

```
  368,734
  198,049
+ 274,376
───────────
```

IXL.com
skill ID
ZMC

Let's Learn!

You can use the following steps to subtract. Look at the example. Remember to regroup.

$$
\begin{array}{r}
{\scriptstyle 1\ 14} \\
47,5\cancel{2}\cancel{4} \\
-\ 38,106 \\
\hline
8
\end{array}
\qquad
\begin{array}{r}
{\scriptstyle 1\ 14} \\
47,5\cancel{2}\cancel{4} \\
-\ 38,106 \\
\hline
18
\end{array}
\qquad
\begin{array}{r}
{\scriptstyle 1\ 14} \\
47,5\cancel{2}\cancel{4} \\
-\ 38,106 \\
\hline
418
\end{array}
$$

$$
\begin{array}{r}
{\scriptstyle 3\ 17\quad 1\ 14} \\
\cancel{4}7,5\cancel{2}\cancel{4} \\
-\ 38,106 \\
\hline
9,418
\end{array}
\qquad
\begin{array}{r}
{\scriptstyle 3\ 17\quad 1\ 14} \\
\cancel{4}7,5\cancel{2}\cancel{4} \\
-\ 38,106 \\
\hline
9,418
\end{array}
$$

So, 47,524 − 38,106 = 9,418!

Subtract.

$$
\begin{array}{r}
36,375 \\
-\ 12,642 \\
\hline
\end{array}
\qquad
\begin{array}{r}
52,905 \\
-\ 14,642 \\
\hline
\end{array}
\qquad
\begin{array}{r}
77,511 \\
-\ 32,415 \\
\hline
\end{array}
$$

$$
\begin{array}{r}
63,242 \\
-\ 56,728 \\
\hline
\end{array}
\qquad
\begin{array}{r}
97,432 \\
-\ 28,871 \\
\hline
\end{array}
\qquad
\begin{array}{r}
86,672 \\
-\ 24,913 \\
\hline
\end{array}
$$

Subtract.

$$
\begin{array}{r}
71,270 \\
-32,425 \\
\hline
\end{array}
\qquad
\begin{array}{r}
54,183 \\
-30,365 \\
\hline
\end{array}
\qquad
\begin{array}{r}
41,423 \\
-36,390 \\
\hline
\end{array}
$$

$$
\begin{array}{r}
97,541 \\
-43,663 \\
\hline
\end{array}
\qquad
\begin{array}{r}
82,476 \\
-51,806 \\
\hline
\end{array}
\qquad
\begin{array}{r}
74,203 \\
-25,097 \\
\hline
\end{array}
$$

$$
\begin{array}{r}
433,560 \\
-180,248 \\
\hline
\end{array}
\qquad
\begin{array}{r}
747,852 \\
-433,678 \\
\hline
\end{array}
\qquad
\begin{array}{r}
824,913 \\
-186,672 \\
\hline
\end{array}
$$

$$
\begin{array}{r}
923,139 \\
-637,714 \\
\hline
\end{array}
\qquad
\begin{array}{r}
878,761 \\
-359,584 \\
\hline
\end{array}
$$

Follow the path!

If the answer is less than 200,000, move one square to the left.

If the answer is between 200,000 and 300,000, move one square down.

If the answer is greater than 300,000, move one square to the right.

START ⬇

283,900 − 173,764	780,547 − 479,347	933,114 − 634,790	888,757 − 665,860
614,288 − 490,919	649,696 − 447,932	490,996 − 308,064	541,343 − 356,948
943,158 − 741,852	945,116 − 637,212	823,804 − 519,923	745,029 − 452,645
435,773 − 210,833	1,000,000 − 780,575	841,682 − 644,431	744,297 − 536,927

FINISH ⬇

Subtract to find the smallest answer!

72,092 −42,153	98,261 −37,454	204,374 − 92,296	131,472 − 67,394
239,421 −237,309	**What is the smallest answer on this page?**		657,072 −649,471
127,382 − 97,456	_____		841,053 −639,844
451,928 −427,392	163,008 − 71,753	640,859 −619,779	785,148 −767,093

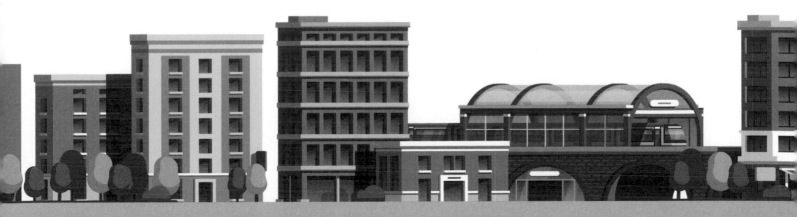

Add or subtract.

$$
\begin{array}{r}
757{,}545 \\
-\,148{,}963 \\
\hline
\end{array}
\qquad
\begin{array}{r}
284{,}991 \\
+\,452{,}568 \\
\hline
\end{array}
\qquad
\begin{array}{r}
885{,}027 \\
-\,310{,}459 \\
\hline
\end{array}
$$

$$
\begin{array}{r}
385{,}920 \\
+\,488{,}986 \\
\hline
\end{array}
\qquad
\begin{array}{r}
738{,}060 \\
-\,455{,}853 \\
\hline
\end{array}
\qquad
\begin{array}{r}
368{,}691 \\
+\,497{,}483 \\
\hline
\end{array}
$$

$$
\begin{array}{r}
433{,}951 \\
-\,178{,}304 \\
\hline
\end{array}
\qquad
\begin{array}{r}
690{,}467 \\
+\,258{,}658 \\
\hline
\end{array}
\qquad
\begin{array}{r}
746{,}206 \\
-\,619{,}739 \\
\hline
\end{array}
$$

Add or subtract to complete the puzzle.

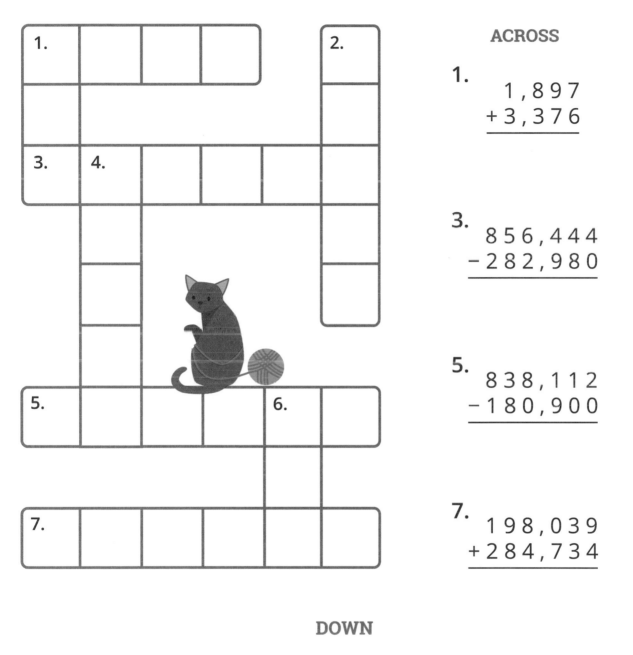

ACROSS

1.
$$\begin{array}{r} 1{,}897 \\ +\,3{,}376 \\ \hline \end{array}$$

3.
$$\begin{array}{r} 856{,}444 \\ -\,282{,}980 \\ \hline \end{array}$$

5.
$$\begin{array}{r} 838{,}112 \\ -\,180{,}900 \\ \hline \end{array}$$

7.
$$\begin{array}{r} 198{,}039 \\ +\,284{,}734 \\ \hline \end{array}$$

DOWN

1.
$$\begin{array}{r} 937{,}034 \\ -\,936{,}489 \\ \hline \end{array}$$

2.
$$\begin{array}{r} 19{,}278 \\ +\,26{,}153 \\ \hline \end{array}$$

4.
$$\begin{array}{r} 15{,}692 \\ +\,54{,}673 \\ \hline \end{array}$$

6.
$$\begin{array}{r} 59{,}106 \\ -\,58{,}989 \\ \hline \end{array}$$

Add or subtract. Compare the answers using >, <, or =.

384,283 + 352,374 ⓒ 317,273 + 456,388

$$
\begin{array}{r}
\overset{1}{3}8\overset{1}{4},283 \\
+\ 352,374 \\
\hline
736,657
\end{array}
\qquad
\begin{array}{r}
\overset{1}{3}17,\overset{1}{2}\overset{1}{7}3 \\
+\ 456,388 \\
\hline
773,661
\end{array}
$$

736,657 < 773,661

521,546 + 117,900 ◯ 98,786 + 543,480

592,482 − 285,617 ◯ 622,920 − 318,422

867,619 − 623,699 ◯ 734,635 − 433,890

Answer each question.

The strawberry shortcake stand at the Plymouth
Strawberry Festival sold 3,166 shortcakes on Saturday.
On Sunday, the stand sold 2,941 shortcakes. How many
shortcakes did the stand sell over the weekend?

_____

Mr. Taylor went skydiving. He jumped when the plane
was 13,780 feet above the ground. Thirty seconds later,
he was 5,492 feet from the ground. How far did he
travel in those thirty seconds?

_____

In its first year of business, Gum Drop Pops made
195,500 lollipops. In its second year of business, the
company made 470,000 lollipops. How many more
lollipops did Gum Drop Pops make in its second year
than in its first year?

_____

Cathy's fourth-grade class visited a recycling center. She
learned that the center collected 217,847 bottles and
89,462 cans last year. How many items is that in all?

_____

Total Thrills Theme Park had 735,032 visitors over the
summer. If 397,217 visitors were children, how many of
the visitors were adults?

_____

Answer each question.

The Spring Harbor Aquarium has 40,780 sea creatures. There are 18,207 fish and 1,279 jellyfish. How many of the creatures at the aquarium are **not** fish or jellyfish?

_____

Pioneer Stadium can hold 54,000 people. At the game today, there are 29,719 fans sitting on the lower deck and 20,387 fans sitting on the upper deck. If there are only two decks, how many empty seats are there?

_____

An empty airplane weighs 87,200 pounds. The weight of the passengers and luggage on the next flight is 43,750 pounds. The weight of the jet fuel for the next flight is 38,900 pounds. How much will the airplane weigh when it has been loaded with passengers, luggage, and jet fuel for the next flight?

_____

A baseball player made $1,000,000 in three years. He made $289,000 during his first year and $325,000 during his second year. How much money did he earn during the third year?

_____

IXL.com
skill ID
9X2

Write the missing numbers. Follow the example.

___3___ rows of ___4___ = ___12___

___3___ × ___4___ = ___12___

_____ rows of _____ = _____

_____ × _____ = _____

_____ rows of _____ = _____

_____ × _____ = _____

_____ rows of _____ = _____

_____ × _____ = _____

_____ rows of _____ = _____

_____ × _____ = _____

IXL.com
skill ID

HZL

Keep it going! Write the missing numbers.

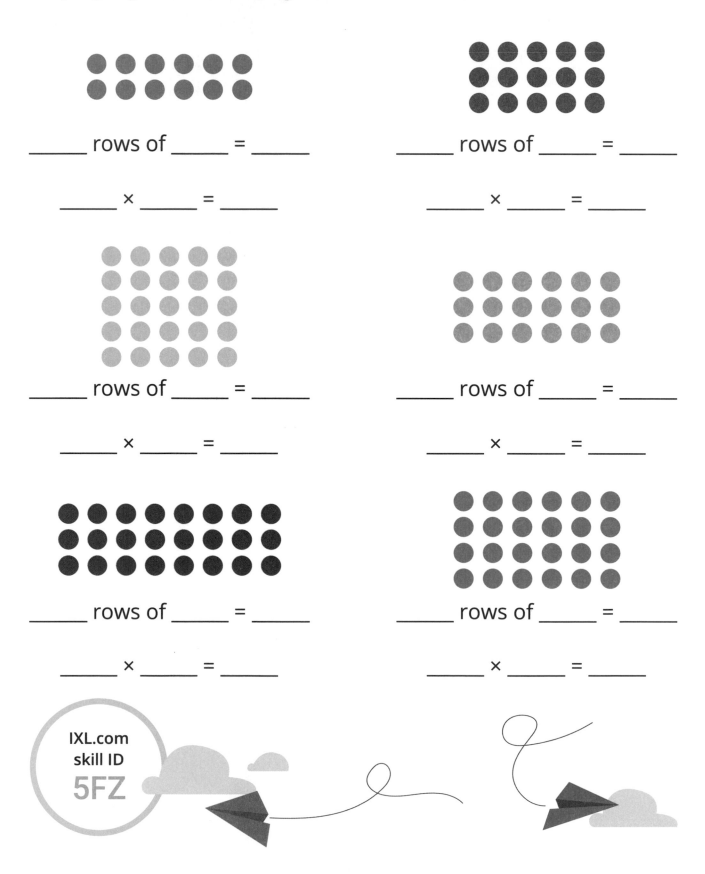

_____ rows of _____ = _____

_____ × _____ = _____

_____ rows of _____ = _____

_____ × _____ = _____

_____ rows of _____ = _____

_____ × _____ = _____

_____ rows of _____ = _____

_____ × _____ = _____

_____ rows of _____ = _____

_____ × _____ = _____

_____ rows of _____ = _____

_____ × _____ = _____

Multiply.

3 × 7 = _____   5 × 4 = _____   4 × 7 = _____

10 × 11 = _____   6 × 12 = _____   1 × 9 = _____

12 × 0 = _____   10 × 2 = _____   9 × 6 = _____

5 × 10 = _____   8 × 4 = _____   6 × 11 = _____

3 × 2 = _____   7 × 8 = _____   9 × 7 = _____

Multiply.

$1 \times 5 =$ _____ $7 \times 6 =$ _____ $10 \times 7 =$ _____

$4 \times 9 =$ _____ $12 \times 3 =$ _____ $2 \times 9 =$ _____

$11 \times 8 =$ _____ $5 \times 8 =$ _____ $4 \times 4 =$ _____

$8 \times 9 =$ _____ $6 \times 5 =$ _____ $2 \times 12 =$ _____

$3 \times 10 =$ _____ $8 \times 3 =$ _____ $6 \times 8 =$ _____

IXL.com
skill ID
FW9

Fill in the blanks. Multiply the two inner numbers to get the outer number.

Write the missing numbers.

2 × _____ = 16   6 × _____ = 42   _____ × 10 = 60

_____ × 4 = 4   7 × _____ = 84   _____ × 5 = 60

7 × _____ = 0   _____ × 12 = 24   10 × _____ = 100

11 × _____ = 22   4 × _____ = 44   _____ × 8 = 64

7 × _____ = 28   _____ × 6 = 48   _____ × 9 = 45

_____ × 12 = 36   _____ × 7 = 56   5 × _____ = 30

IXL.com
skill ID
76F

Answer each question.

Sophia is 9 years old. Her grandpa is 6 times as old as she is. How old is Sophia's grandpa?

_____

Harold's neighborhood organized a cleanup day. The volunteers split up into 8 groups with 5 people in each group. How many volunteers were there in all?

_____

Jacob is cutting 9 apples for an apple pie. He cuts each apple into 8 slices. How many apple slices is that in all?

_____

Isabella and Elijah took an origami class over the summer. Isabella made 9 paper cranes in the class. Elijah made 3 times as many paper cranes as Isabella. How many paper cranes did Elijah make?

_____

There are 12 tables in the art room at the community center. There are 8 seats at each table. How many people can fit at all of the tables in the art room?

_____

> **Let's Learn!**
>
> You can use multiplication facts to help multiply by multiples of 10. You can think of the problems like this:
>
> | 4 × 30 | 4 × 300 |
> |---|---|
> | 4 × 3 tens | 4 × 3 hundreds |
> | 12 tens | 12 hundreds |
> | 120 | 1,200 |

Multiply.

7 × 40 = _____

2 × 60 = _____

6 × 600 = _____

6 × 300 = _____

3 × 5,000 = _____

9 × 60 = _____

8 × 2,000 = _____

4 × 90,000 = _____

7 × 7,000 = _____

4 × 40,000 = _____

5 × 6,000 = _____

You can round to estimate the answer to a multiplication problem. Estimate by rounding the second factor to the nearest ten.

4 × 17 is about 4 × ___20___ = ___80___

7 × 29 is about 7 × _____ = _____

9 × 53 is about 9 × _____ = _____

2 × 72 is about 2 × _____ = _____

6 × 37 is about 6 × _____ = _____

8 × 81 is about 8 × _____ = _____

5 × 41 is about 5 × _____ = _____

3 × 98 is about 3 × _____ = _____

IXL.com
skill ID
WDG

Let's Learn!

You can break up numbers to make them easier to multiply. Try it for 4 × 63.

$4 × 63 = 4 × (60 + 3)$ Start by writing 63 as 60 + 3.

$4 × 63 = (4 × 60) + (4 × 3)$ Multiply 4 by 60, and multiply 4 by 3.

$4 × 63 = 240 + 12$ Then add the two products.

$4 × 63 = 252$ So, 4 × 63 is 252!

Fill in the blanks.

Pick numbers that are easy to multiply, like multiples of 10.

$6 × 37 = 6 × (\underline{\hspace{1cm} 30 \hspace{1cm}} + \underline{\hspace{1cm} 7 \hspace{1cm}})$

$6 × 37 = (6 × \underline{\hspace{1cm} 30 \hspace{1cm}}) + (6 × \underline{\hspace{1cm} 7 \hspace{1cm}})$

$6 × 37 = \underline{\hspace{1cm} 180 \hspace{1cm}} + \underline{\hspace{1cm} 42 \hspace{1cm}}$

$6 × 37 = \underline{\hspace{1cm} 222 \hspace{1cm}}$

$9 × 52 = 9 × (\underline{\hspace{2cm}} + \underline{\hspace{2cm}})$

$9 × 52 = (9 × \underline{\hspace{2cm}}) + (9 × \underline{\hspace{2cm}})$

$9 × 52 = \underline{\hspace{2cm}} + \underline{\hspace{2cm}}$

$9 × 52 = \underline{\hspace{2cm}}$

Fill in the blanks.

5 × 87 = 5 × (_____ + _____)

5 × 87 = (5 × _____) + (5 × _____)

5 × 87 = _____ + _____

5 × 87 = _____

7 × 29 = 7 × (_____ + _____)

7 × 29 = (7 × _____) + (7 × _____)

7 × 29 = _____ + _____

7 × 29 = _____

4 × 95 = 4 × (_____ + _____)

4 × 95 = (4 × _____) + (4 × _____)

4 × 95 = _____ + _____

4 × 95 = _____

Try it for larger numbers! Fill in the blanks.

5 × 325 = 5 × (__300__ + __20__ + __5__)

5 × 325 = (5 × __300__) + (5 × __20__) + (5 × __5__)

5 × 325 = __1,500__ + __100__ + __25__

5 × 325 = __1,625__

3 × 654 = 3 × (_____ + _____ + _____)

3 × 654 = (3 × _____) + (3 × _____) + (3 × _____)

3 × 654 = _____ + _____ + _____

3 × 654 = _____

7 × 263 = 7 × (_____ + _____ + _____)

7 × 263 = (7 × _____) + (7 × _____) + (7 × _____)

7 × 263 = _____ + _____ + _____

7 × 263 = _____

Keep going! Multiply.

$4 \times 57 = \underline{\quad 228 \quad}$

$4 \times (50 + 7)$
$(4 \times 50) + (4 \times 7)$
$200 + 28 = 228$

$7 \times 48 = \underline{\qquad\qquad}$

$8 \times 39 = \underline{\qquad\qquad}$

$6 \times 72 = \underline{\qquad\qquad}$

$4 \times 154 = \underline{\qquad\qquad}$

$3 \times 293 = \underline{\qquad\qquad}$

$9 \times 244 = \underline{\qquad\qquad}$

$7 \times 518 = \underline{\qquad\qquad}$

Let's Learn!

You can use place value to multiply larger numbers. For example, try it with 72 × 4.

First, multiply the **ones**.

$$\begin{array}{r} 7\,2 \\ \times\ \ \ 4 \\ \hline 8 \end{array}$$

2 ones × 4 = 8 ones

Then, multiply the **tens**.

$$\begin{array}{r} 7\,2 \\ \times\ \ \ 4 \\ \hline 2\,8\,8 \end{array}$$

7 tens × 4 = 28 tens

28 tens = 2 hundreds and 8 tens

So, 72 × 4 is 288!

Multiply.

$$\begin{array}{r} 4\,1 \\ \times\ \ 5 \\ \hline 2\,0\,5 \end{array}$$

$$\begin{array}{r} 3\,4 \\ \times\ \ 2 \\ \hline \end{array}$$

$$\begin{array}{r} 9\,1 \\ \times\ \ 4 \\ \hline \end{array}$$

$$\begin{array}{r} 8\,3 \\ \times\ \ 2 \\ \hline \end{array}$$

$$\begin{array}{r} 2\,3 \\ \times\ \ 3 \\ \hline \end{array}$$

$$\begin{array}{r} 2\,1 \\ \times\ \ 8 \\ \hline \end{array}$$

Multiply.

$$\begin{array}{r} 9\,4 \\ \times\ \ 2 \\ \hline \end{array}$$

$$\begin{array}{r} 6\,1 \\ \times\ \ 5 \\ \hline \end{array}$$

$$\begin{array}{r} 5\,1 \\ \times\ \ 7 \\ \hline \end{array}$$

$$\begin{array}{r} 8\,2 \\ \times\ \ 4 \\ \hline \end{array}$$

$$\begin{array}{r} 5\,4 \\ \times\ \ 2 \\ \hline \end{array}$$

$$\begin{array}{r} 7\,2 \\ \times\ \ 3 \\ \hline \end{array}$$

$$\begin{array}{r} 6\,1 \\ \times\ \ 9 \\ \hline \end{array}$$

$$\begin{array}{r} 7\,1 \\ \times\ \ 8 \\ \hline \end{array}$$

$$\begin{array}{r} 6\,2 \\ \times\ \ 4 \\ \hline \end{array}$$

$$\begin{array}{r} 5\,3 \\ \times\ \ 3 \\ \hline \end{array}$$

$$\begin{array}{r} 6\,4 \\ \times\ \ 2 \\ \hline \end{array}$$

$$\begin{array}{r} 8\,1 \\ \times\ \ 6 \\ \hline \end{array}$$

Let's Learn!

When multiplying larger numbers, sometimes you have to regroup. Try it with 54 × 6.

First, multiply the **ones**.

```
    2
  5 4
×   6
─────
    4
```

4 ones × 6 = 24 ones

24 ones = 2 tens and 4 ones

Write the ones below. Write the tens above to save them for the next step.

Then, multiply the **tens**.

```
    2
  5 4
×   6
─────
3 2 4
```

5 tens × 6 = 30 tens

Add the extra 2 tens you saved at the top.

30 tens + 2 tens = 32 tens

32 tens = 3 hundreds and 2 tens

So, 54 × 6 is 324!

Multiply.

```
  1
  6 3
× 5
─────
3 1 5
```

```
  4 8
× 2
─────
```

```
  3 7
× 3
─────
```

```
  4 6
× 5
─────
```

```
  8 6
× 4
─────
```

```
  9 7
× 8
─────
```

Multiply.

$$\begin{array}{r} 43 \\ \times\ 4 \\ \hline \end{array}$$

$$\begin{array}{r} 82 \\ \times\ 7 \\ \hline \end{array}$$

$$\begin{array}{r} 19 \\ \times\ 5 \\ \hline \end{array}$$

$$\begin{array}{r} 35 \\ \times\ 8 \\ \hline \end{array}$$

$$\begin{array}{r} 38 \\ \times\ 3 \\ \hline \end{array}$$

$$\begin{array}{r} 26 \\ \times\ 6 \\ \hline \end{array}$$

$$\begin{array}{r} 29 \\ \times\ 9 \\ \hline \end{array}$$

$$\begin{array}{r} 53 \\ \times\ 7 \\ \hline \end{array}$$

$$\begin{array}{r} 45 \\ \times\ 4 \\ \hline \end{array}$$

$$\begin{array}{r} 65 \\ \times\ 5 \\ \hline \end{array}$$

$$\begin{array}{r} 84 \\ \times\ 6 \\ \hline \end{array}$$

IXL.com
skill ID
GDW

Keep it going with larger numbers! Multiply.

```
  1
  5 6 3          4 3 3          7 0 2
×     3        ×     2        ×     4
─────────      ─────────      ─────────
1,689
```

```
  9 4 2          2 0 3          8 2 4
×     4        ×     8        ×     5
─────────      ─────────      ─────────
```

```
  5 3 2          1 7 3          6 0 8
×     6        ×     9        ×     7
─────────      ─────────      ─────────
```

```
  8 3 7          7 5 4          3 8 5
×     6        ×     8        ×     9
─────────      ─────────      ─────────
```

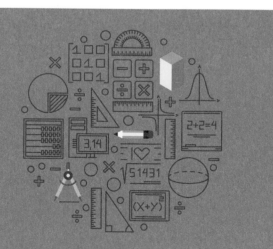

Multiply.

$$\begin{array}{r} 319 \\ \times \quad 4 \\ \hline \end{array}$$

$$\begin{array}{r} 335 \\ \times \quad 3 \\ \hline \end{array}$$

$$\begin{array}{r} 509 \\ \times \quad 2 \\ \hline \end{array}$$

$$\begin{array}{r} 625 \\ \times \quad 6 \\ \hline \end{array}$$

$$\begin{array}{r} 623 \\ \times \quad 8 \\ \hline \end{array}$$

$$\begin{array}{r} 718 \\ \times \quad 5 \\ \hline \end{array}$$

$$\begin{array}{r} 407 \\ \times \quad 7 \\ \hline \end{array}$$

$$\begin{array}{r} 257 \\ \times \quad 9 \\ \hline \end{array}$$

$$\begin{array}{r} 876 \\ \times \quad 4 \\ \hline \end{array}$$

$$\begin{array}{r} 674 \\ \times \quad 7 \\ \hline \end{array}$$

$$\begin{array}{r} 795 \\ \times \quad 5 \\ \hline \end{array}$$

$$\begin{array}{r} 494 \\ \times \quad 3 \\ \hline \end{array}$$

IXL.com
skill ID
FA7

Multiply.

$$\begin{array}{r} \overset{1}{3,841} \\ \times\qquad 2 \\ \hline 7,682 \end{array}$$

$$\begin{array}{r} 5,132 \\ \times\qquad 4 \\ \hline \end{array}$$

$$\begin{array}{r} 3,812 \\ \times\qquad 5 \\ \hline \end{array}$$

$$\begin{array}{r} 5,192 \\ \times\qquad 3 \\ \hline \end{array}$$

$$\begin{array}{r} 1,872 \\ \times\qquad 8 \\ \hline \end{array}$$

$$\begin{array}{r} 1,453 \\ \times\qquad 7 \\ \hline \end{array}$$

$$\begin{array}{r} 2,654 \\ \times\qquad 6 \\ \hline \end{array}$$

$$\begin{array}{r} 4,639 \\ \times\qquad 9 \\ \hline \end{array}$$

$$\begin{array}{r} 3,762 \\ \times\qquad 4 \\ \hline \end{array}$$

$$\begin{array}{r} 6,725 \\ \times\qquad 5 \\ \hline \end{array}$$

$$\begin{array}{r} 5,913 \\ \times\qquad 8 \\ \hline \end{array}$$

$$\begin{array}{r} 6,670 \\ \times\qquad 3 \\ \hline \end{array}$$

$$\begin{array}{r} 3,943 \\ \times\qquad 6 \\ \hline \end{array}$$

$$\begin{array}{r} 7,527 \\ \times\qquad 9 \\ \hline \end{array}$$

IXL.com
skill ID
PPM

William, Olivia, Emma, Jayden, and Noah are running in a race. Each runner is assigned a race number. Use the clues to solve the logic puzzle.

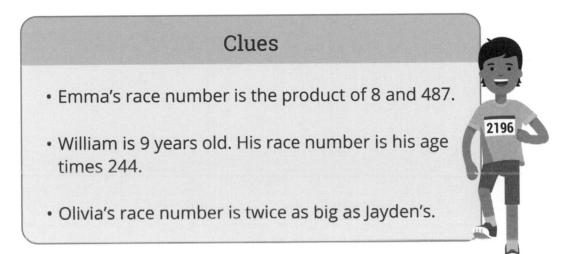

Clues

- Emma's race number is the product of 8 and 487.

- William is 9 years old. His race number is his age times 244.

- Olivia's race number is twice as big as Jayden's.

Race number	William	Olivia	Emma	Jayden	Noah
1,286					
1,770					
2,196					
3,540					
3,896					

Answer each question.

Ava sold 28 bags of popcorn for a fundraiser. Michael sold 3 times as many bags of popcorn as Ava did. How many bags of popcorn did Michael sell?

_____

Ethan is in charge of setting up the Summerdale Chili Cook-Off. He bought 7 packages of paper bowls. Each package has 25 bowls. How many bowls did Ethan buy?

_____

The Natural History Museum has 92 plant fossils. The museum has 4 times as many animal fossils as plant fossils. How many animal fossils does the museum have?

_____

At a hockey rink, there are 8 sections of seats with 164 seats in each section. How many total seats are at the hockey rink?

_____

There are 5,280 feet in a mile. How many feet are in 3 miles?

_____

IXL.com
skill ID
7NS

Let's Learn!

When you multiply multiples of 10, you can think of the problems like this:

70 × 30	50 × 60
70 × 3 tens	50 × 6 tens
210 tens	300 tens
2,100	3,000

Multiply.

20 × 30 = __600__   40 × 60 = _____   80 × 20 = _____

50 × 70 = _____   30 × 30 = _____   80 × 60 = _____

80 × 80 = _____   90 × 60 = _____   40 × 70 = _____

90 × 40 = _____   80 × 50 = _____   70 × 90 = _____

Let's Learn!

You can use place value to multiply two-digit numbers. Try it for 43 × 65. To start, take the first number and multiply it by the ones digit of the second number. In this example, multiply 43 × 5.

$$
\begin{array}{r}
1 \\
4\,3 \\
\times\ 6\,5 \\
\hline
5
\end{array}
\qquad\rightarrow\qquad
\begin{array}{r}
1 \\
4\,3 \\
\times\ \ 6\,5 \\
\hline
2\,1\,5
\end{array}
$$

Remember to regroup 15 into 1 ten and 5 ones.

Remember to add the 1 ten that you regrouped.

Next, multiply the first number by the tens digit of the second number. In this example, multiply 43 × 6. Write the numbers below the 215.

$$
\begin{array}{r}
1 \\
4\,3 \\
\times\ \ 6\,5 \\
\hline
2\,1\,5 \\
8\,0
\end{array}
\ \rightarrow\
\begin{array}{r}
1 \\
4\,3 \\
\times\ \ 6\,5 \\
\hline
2\,1\,5 \\
2,5\,8\,0
\end{array}
\ \rightarrow\
\begin{array}{r}
1 \\
4\,3 \\
\times\ \ 6\,5 \\
\hline
2\,1\,5 \\
+\,2,5\,8\,0 \\
\hline
2,7\,9\,5
\end{array}
$$

Because the 6 represents tens, the numbers will start in the tens column. Put a 0 in the ones column.

Multiply 6 tens × 3 ones. Remember to regroup 18 tens into 8 tens and 1 hundred.

Multiply 6 tens × 4 tens, and then add the 1 hundred you regrouped.

Add 215 + 2,580 to get the final product!

Multiply.

$$
\begin{array}{r}
2 \\
2\,7 \\
\times\,1\,3 \\
\hline
8\,1 \\
+\,2\,7\,0 \\
\hline
3\,5\,1
\end{array}
\qquad\qquad
\begin{array}{r}
8\,1 \\
\times\,7\,4 \\
\hline
\end{array}
\qquad\qquad
\begin{array}{r}
5\,2 \\
\times\,3\,8 \\
\hline
\end{array}
$$

Keep going! Multiply.

$$\begin{array}{r} 41 \\ \times\,26 \\ \hline \end{array} \qquad \begin{array}{r} 14 \\ \times\,34 \\ \hline \end{array} \qquad \begin{array}{r} 45 \\ \times\,46 \\ \hline \end{array}$$

$$\begin{array}{r} 92 \\ \times\,54 \\ \hline \end{array} \qquad \begin{array}{r} 75 \\ \times\,61 \\ \hline \end{array} \qquad \begin{array}{r} 62 \\ \times\,16 \\ \hline \end{array}$$

$$\begin{array}{r} 22 \\ \times\,97 \\ \hline \end{array} \qquad \begin{array}{r} 76 \\ \times\,32 \\ \hline \end{array} \qquad \begin{array}{r} 36 \\ \times\,53 \\ \hline \end{array}$$

Multiply.

$$\begin{array}{r} 35 \\ \times\, 42 \\ \hline \end{array}$$ $$\begin{array}{r} 29 \\ \times\, 85 \\ \hline \end{array}$$ $$\begin{array}{r} 84 \\ \times\, 43 \\ \hline \end{array}$$

$$\begin{array}{r} 73 \\ \times\, 37 \\ \hline \end{array}$$ $$\begin{array}{r} 27 \\ \times\, 58 \\ \hline \end{array}$$ $$\begin{array}{r} 39 \\ \times\, 57 \\ \hline \end{array}$$

$$\begin{array}{r} 79 \\ \times\, 46 \\ \hline \end{array}$$ $$\begin{array}{r} 49 \\ \times\, 65 \\ \hline \end{array}$$ $$\begin{array}{r} 68 \\ \times\, 44 \\ \hline \end{array}$$

$$\begin{array}{r} 67 \\ \times\, 93 \\ \hline \end{array}$$ $$\begin{array}{r} 77 \\ \times\, 64 \\ \hline \end{array}$$ $$\begin{array}{r} 83 \\ \times\, 92 \\ \hline \end{array}$$

IXL.com
skill ID
MLC

Answer each question.

The owner of Howie's Hamburger Wagon bought 18 packs of hamburger buns. There were 24 buns in each pack. How many hamburger buns did he buy?

_____

Julie bought a photo book. It has 36 pages, and each page holds 16 photos. How many photos can the photo book hold?

_____

Sam is helping his uncle store bags of horse feed in his stables. A bag of horse feed weighs 25 pounds. Sam's uncle bought 12 bags of horse feed. How many pounds of horse feed is that in all?

_____

Madison's class took a field trip to the zoo. Each person's ticket cost $18. If 21 people went on the field trip, what was the total cost of admission?

_____

Summer Street Bakery uses 47 marshmallows in each of its famous s'mores cakes. How many marshmallows will the bakery need to complete an order for 32 s'mores cakes?

_____

Answer each question.

Shannon sells her homemade pottery at craft fairs. She sells vases for $12 and planters for $16. This weekend, she sold 22 vases and 17 planters in total. Did Shannon make more money selling vases or planters?

_____

Mr. Bailey is setting up chairs for a play. He sets up 47 rows of chairs. Each row has 26 chairs. He puts one more row with 13 chairs in the back of the auditorium. How many total chairs does he set up?

_____

During summer break, Chloe made $18 every day she walked her neighbor's dogs. She worked 39 days over the summer. After she got paid, she spent $187 on new ski boots. How much money did Chloe have left over?

_____

A comic book store has 32 racks that each hold 96 comic books. All of the racks are full except one rack that has 89 comic books. How many comic books are there in all?

_____

IXL.com
skill ID
GZG

Write a multiplication equation and a division equation for each model.

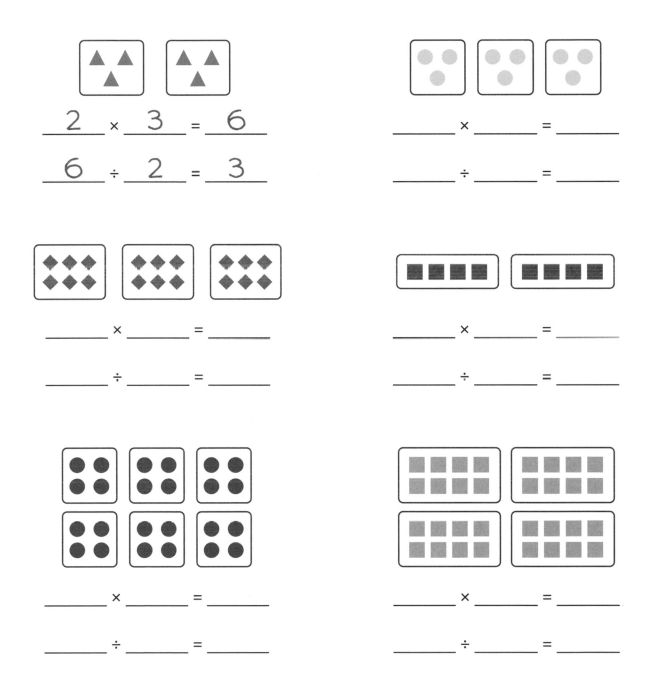

___2___ × ___3___ = ___6___

___6___ ÷ ___2___ = ___3___

_____ × _____ = _____

_____ ÷ _____ = _____

_____ × _____ = _____

_____ ÷ _____ = _____

_____ × _____ = _____

_____ ÷ _____ = _____

_____ × _____ = _____

_____ ÷ _____ = _____

_____ × _____ = _____

_____ ÷ _____ = _____

Divide.

$12 \div 4 =$ ___3___ $22 \div 2 =$ _____ $10 \div 5 =$ _____

$18 \div 2 =$ _____ $30 \div 6 =$ _____ $25 \div 5 =$ _____

$28 \div 4 =$ _____ $50 \div 10 =$ _____ $14 \div 2 =$ _____

$64 \div 8 =$ _____ $8 \div 1 =$ _____ $40 \div 10 =$ _____

$21 \div 7 =$ _____ $60 \div 6 =$ _____ $24 \div 12 =$ _____

Divide.

$12 \div 2 =$ _____ $7 \div 7 =$ _____ $54 \div 9 =$ _____

$32 \div 4 =$ _____ $120 \div 12 =$ _____ $27 \div 3 =$ _____

$99 \div 11 =$ _____ $36 \div 9 =$ _____ $84 \div 12 =$ _____

$35 \div 5 =$ _____ $18 \div 3 =$ _____ $110 \div 10 =$ _____

$30 \div 10 =$ _____ $72 \div 12 =$ _____ $28 \div 7 =$ _____

$42 \div 6 =$ _____ $81 \div 9 =$ _____ $40 \div 8 =$ _____

IXL.com
skill ID
R95

Write the missing numbers.

60 ÷ __12__ = 5   _____ ÷ 5 = 1   22 ÷ _____ = 2

70 ÷ _____ = 7   _____ ÷ 4 = 2   20 ÷ _____ = 5

20 ÷ _____ = 10   _____ ÷ 5 = 8   66 ÷ _____ = 11

63 ÷ _____ = 9   24 ÷ _____ = 8   _____ ÷ 4 = 9

_____ ÷ 1 = 6   84 ÷ _____ = 12   88 ÷ _____ = 8

_____ ÷ 9 = 5   108 ÷ _____ = 9   16 ÷ _____ = 8

_____ ÷ 4 = 12   30 ÷ _____ = 6   _____ ÷ 10 = 11

Answer each question.

Patrick is designing his school's yearbook. He has
72 pictures left and 8 blank pages to fill. If he wants to
put the same number of pictures on each remaining
page, how many pictures will go on each page?

_____

Natalie scored 3 times as many soccer goals this
season as last season. If she scored 12 goals this
season, how many goals did she score last season?

_____

Bella's Bakery has two cupcake orders this morning.
The first order is for 42 cupcakes. It has 6 times as
many cupcakes as the second order. How many
cupcakes are in the second order?

_____

The guests at Lisa's birthday party are splitting up into
teams of 6 to play a game. If there are 24 guests at the
party, how many teams will there be?

_____

Pete's grandma has her own recipes for banana pudding and banana bread.
The pudding recipe calls for 7 times as many bananas as the bread recipe. If the
pudding recipe calls for 14 bananas, how many
bananas are needed for the bread recipe?

_____

IXL.com
skill ID
XZA

Let's Learn!

When you divide multiples of 10, you can think of the problems like this:

720 ÷ 8

72 tens ÷ 8

9 tens

90

7,200 ÷ 8

72 hundreds ÷ 8

9 hundreds

900

Divide.

1,800 ÷ 2 = _____

330 ÷ 11 = _____

21,000 ÷ 3 = _____

36,000 ÷ 6 = _____

4,200 ÷ 7 = _____

160 ÷ 4 = _____

25,000 ÷ 5 = _____

2,400 ÷ 3 = _____

840 ÷ 12 = _____

40,000 ÷ 8 = _____

770 ÷ 7 = _____

IXL.com
skill ID
2K3

Let's Learn!

You can use division with multiples of 10 to estimate quotients. Try it with 378 ÷ 6. Think about 378. What nearby multiples of 10 can you divide by 6? You can divide 360 and 420 by 6.

$$360 \div 6 = 60$$

$$420 \div 6 = 70$$

So, 378 ÷ 6 must be between 60 and 70.

Estimate each quotient. Fill in the blanks with the nearest multiples of 10.

315 ÷ 7 is between __40__ and __50__.   135 ÷ 9 is between _____ and _____.

$$280 \div 7 = 40$$
$$350 \div 7 = 50$$

264 ÷ 6 is between _____ and _____.   475 ÷ 5 is between _____ and _____.

448 ÷ 8 is between _____ and _____.   234 ÷ 3 is between _____ and _____.

450 ÷ 6 is between _____ and _____.   444 ÷ 12 is between _____ and _____.

Let's Learn!

You can split bigger numbers into smaller numbers to make it easier to divide. Let's try it for 138 ÷ 6!

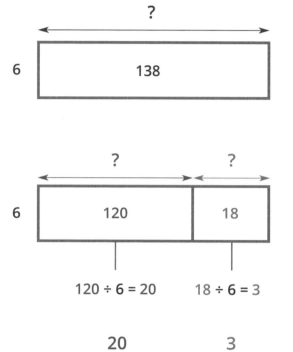

Split 138 into smaller numbers. For example, 138 is 120 + 18.

So, 138 ÷ 6 = (120 + 18) ÷ 6.

Divide each smaller number by 6.

So, 138 ÷ 6 = (120 ÷ 6) + (18 ÷ 6).

Find the sum.

138 ÷ 6 = 20 + 3 = 23

So, 138 ÷ 6 = 23!

You can split numbers however you want. For example, you could have split 138 into 60 + 60 + 18. In general, it is best to choose numbers that divide easily.

Fill in the blanks.

162 ÷ 3 = (150 + 12) ÷ 3

162 ÷ 3 = (__150__ ÷ __3__) + (__12__ ÷ __3__)

162 ÷ 3 = __50__ + __4__

162 ÷ 3 = __54__

364 ÷ 7 = (350 + 14) ÷ 7

364 ÷ 7 = (_____ ÷ _____) + (_____ ÷ _____)

364 ÷ 7 = _____ + _____

364 ÷ 7 = _____

696 ÷ 8 = (640 + 56) ÷ 8

696 ÷ 8 = (_____ ÷ _____) + (_____ ÷ _____)

696 ÷ 8 = _____ + _____

696 ÷ 8 = _____

Fill in the blanks.

152 ÷ 4 = (_____ + _____) ÷ _____

152 ÷ 4 = (_____ ÷ _____) + (_____ ÷ _____)

152 ÷ 4 = _____ + _____

152 ÷ 4 = _____

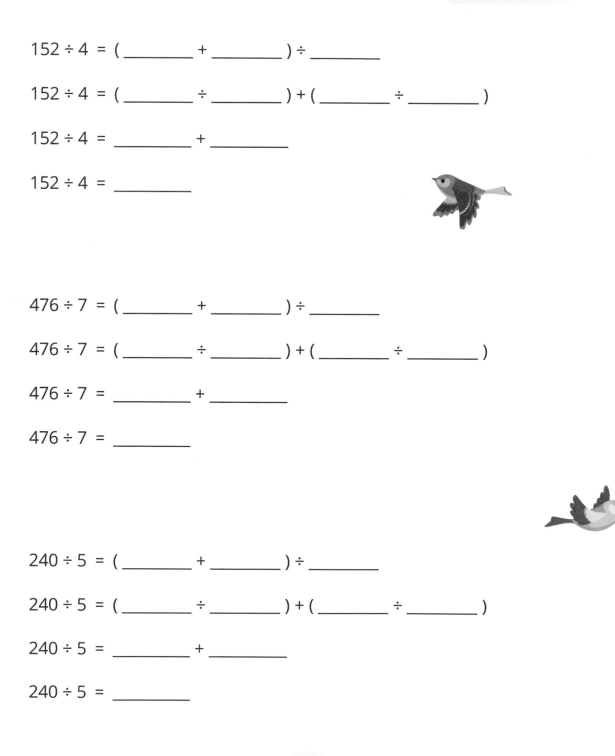

476 ÷ 7 = (_____ + _____) ÷ _____

476 ÷ 7 = (_____ ÷ _____) + (_____ ÷ _____)

476 ÷ 7 = _____ + _____

476 ÷ 7 = _____

240 ÷ 5 = (_____ + _____) ÷ _____

240 ÷ 5 = (_____ ÷ _____) + (_____ ÷ _____)

240 ÷ 5 = _____ + _____

240 ÷ 5 = _____

Divide. Split the larger number into smaller numbers to help.

$291 ÷ 3 = \underline{\ 97\ }$

$(270 + 21) ÷ 3$

$(270 ÷ 3) + (21 ÷ 3)$

$90 + 7 = 97$

$375 ÷ 5 = \underline{\hspace{1.5cm}}$

$304 ÷ 4 = \underline{\hspace{1.5cm}}$

$581 ÷ 7 = \underline{\hspace{1.5cm}}$

$318 ÷ 6 = \underline{\hspace{1.5cm}}$

$558 ÷ 9 = \underline{\hspace{1.5cm}}$

$768 ÷ 8 = \underline{\hspace{1.5cm}}$

$948 ÷ 12 = \underline{\hspace{1.5cm}}$

IXL.com
skill ID
GDX

Let's Learn!

So far, you've used division facts to help you divide. You can use **long division** to divide, too. Just follow these steps! Here is how to do 97 ÷ 4.

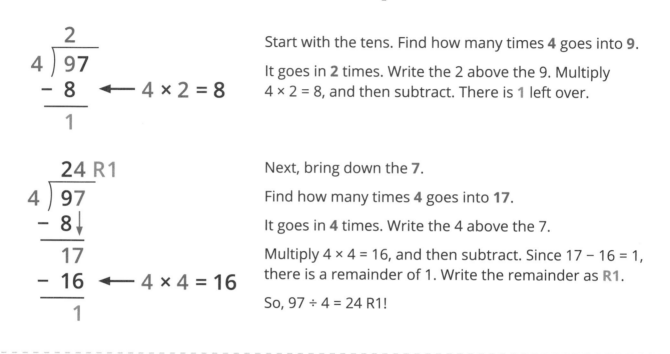

Start with the tens. Find how many times **4** goes into **9**.

It goes in **2** times. Write the 2 above the 9. Multiply 4 × 2 = 8, and then subtract. There is **1** left over.

Next, bring down the **7**.

Find how many times **4** goes into **17**.

It goes in **4** times. Write the 4 above the 7.

Multiply 4 × 4 = 16, and then subtract. Since 17 − 16 = 1, there is a remainder of 1. Write the remainder as **R1**.

So, 97 ÷ 4 = 24 R1!

Divide.

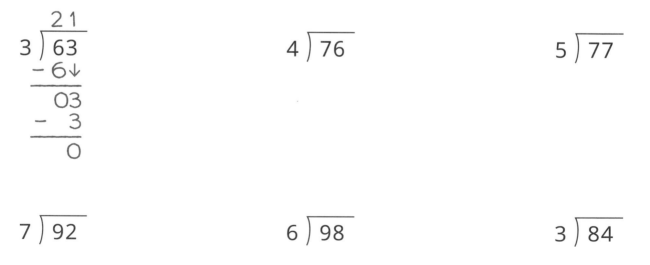

Divide.

$4\overline{)89}$ $\qquad$ $3\overline{)81}$ $\qquad$ $2\overline{)78}$

$3\overline{)71}$ $\qquad$ $5\overline{)95}$ $\qquad$ $8\overline{)98}$

$6\overline{)79}$ $\qquad$ $7\overline{)99}$ $\qquad$ $4\overline{)71}$

Keep it going with larger numbers! Divide.

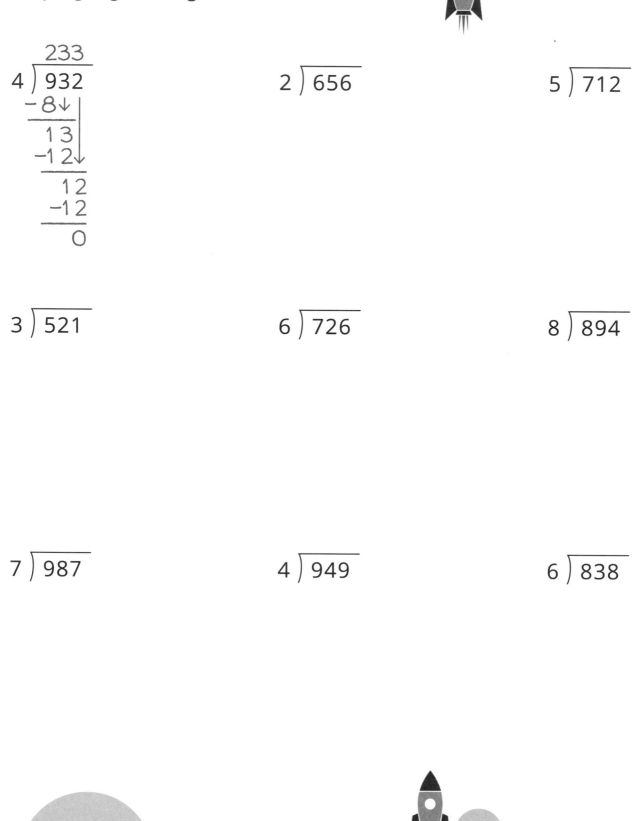

$$
\begin{array}{r}
233 \\
4\overline{)932} \\
-8\downarrow \\
\hline
13 \\
-12\downarrow \\
\hline
12 \\
-12 \\
\hline
0
\end{array}
$$

$2\overline{)656}$

$5\overline{)712}$

$3\overline{)521}$

$6\overline{)726}$

$8\overline{)894}$

$7\overline{)987}$

$4\overline{)949}$

$6\overline{)838}$

Let's Learn!

Sometimes when you divide, you need a 0 in the quotient. Try it for 618 ÷ 3.

$$
\begin{array}{r}
2 \\
3 \overline{)618} \\
-6 \\
\hline
0
\end{array}
$$

← 3 × 2 = 6

Start with the hundreds. Find how many times **3** goes into **6**. Write the answer at the top, and then multiply and subtract.

$$
\begin{array}{r}
206 \\
3 \overline{)618} \\
-6\downarrow\downarrow \\
\hline
018 \\
-18 \\
\hline
0
\end{array}
$$

← 3 × 6 = 18

Next, bring down the **1** in the tens place. Since **3** doesn't go into **1**, write a **0** at the top. Then, move on to divide the ones.

Find out how many times **3** goes into **18**. Write the answer at the top, and then multiply and subtract.

So, 618 ÷ 3 = 206!

If 0 is the first number in the quotient, you don't need to write it down. Check out the first problem below.

Divide.

$$
\begin{array}{r}
45 \\
5 \overline{)225} \\
-20\downarrow \\
\hline
25 \\
-25 \\
\hline
0
\end{array}
$$

$2 \overline{)818}$

$6 \overline{)348}$

$4 \overline{)428}$

$8 \overline{)632}$

$7 \overline{)756}$

Divide.

$5 \overline{)544}$ $4 \overline{)688}$ $3 \overline{)228}$

$6 \overline{)630}$ $7 \overline{)905}$ $9 \overline{)752}$

$4 \overline{)733}$ $6 \overline{)564}$ $8 \overline{)997}$

Divide to complete the puzzle.

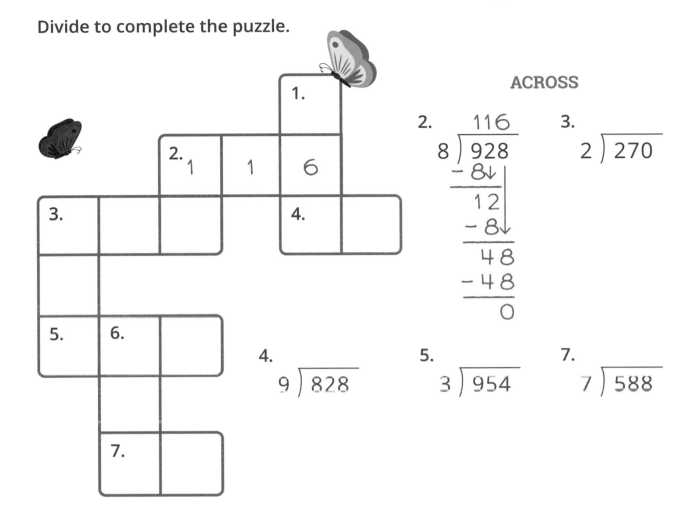

ACROSS

2.
$$\begin{array}{r} 116 \\ 8\overline{)928} \\ -8\downarrow \\ \overline{12} \\ -8\downarrow \\ \overline{48} \\ -48 \\ \overline{0} \end{array}$$

3. $2\overline{)270}$

4. $9\overline{)828}$

5. $3\overline{)954}$

7. $7\overline{)588}$

DOWN

1. $3\overline{)507}$

2. $9\overline{)135}$

3. $4\overline{)772}$

6. $6\overline{)768}$

Divide.

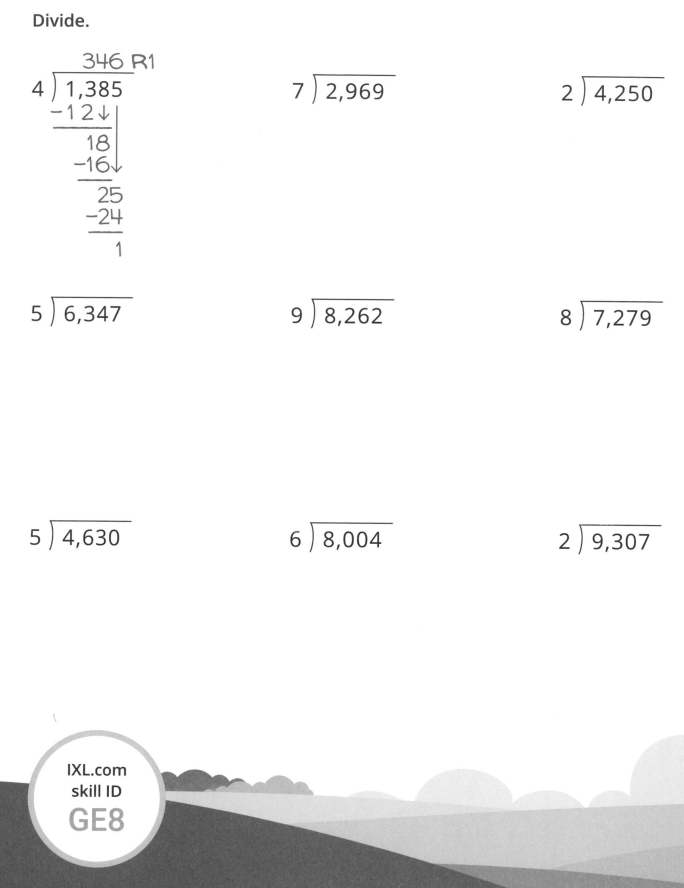

$$346 \text{ R1}$$
$$4\overline{)1,385}$$
$$-12\downarrow$$
$$18$$
$$-16\downarrow$$
$$25$$
$$-24$$
$$1$$

$$7\overline{)2,969}$$

$$2\overline{)4,250}$$

$$5\overline{)6,347}$$

$$9\overline{)8,262}$$

$$8\overline{)7,279}$$

$$5\overline{)4,630}$$

$$6\overline{)8,004}$$

$$2\overline{)9,307}$$

Answer each question.

Mrs. Thomas is making flower arrangements for a wedding. If she has 276 flowers and wants to put 8 flowers in each arrangement, how many arrangements will she be able to make?

_____ flower arrangements with _____ flowers left over

Josh feeds his puppy 3 cups of dog food each day. If a full bag contains 134 cups of dog food, how many days of meals does that cover?

_____ days with _____ cups of dog food left over

The students in Ms. Clark's class are filling treat bags with exactly 8 pieces of candy for the school carnival. If they have 725 pieces of candy in all, how many treat bags can be made?

_____ treat bags with _____ pieces of candy left over

Mr. Green owns a farm. He is planting a pumpkin patch using 240 seeds. He plants the seeds in rows of 9, until he gets to the last row. How many seeds does Mr. Green plant in the last row if he uses all of the seeds?

_____ seeds

In some problems with remainders, you need to round up or down to answer the question. Try it yourself! Answer each question.

There are 95 campers at Pine Castle Summer Camp this week. If each cabin can fit 4 campers, how many cabins are needed?

_____

Lily's grandmother is buying hot dogs for an upcoming family reunion. There are 6 hot dogs in a package. If Lily's grandmother needs 200 hot dogs, how many packages should she buy?

_____

A chef bought a package of 356 cheese sticks to make his famous fried cheese sticks appetizer. If there are 5 cheese sticks in each order, how many orders can the chef make?

_____

Liam leads penguin tours at the aquarium. Today, 178 visitors have signed up for a penguin tour. Tours can take up to 9 visitors. All of the tours for the day are full except for the last one. How many tours will Liam lead today?

_____

At a candy factory, the peanut butter cup machine can make 2,875 peanut butter cups in one hour. There are 8 peanut butter cups in one box. How many boxes of peanut butter cups can be filled in an hour?

_____

Divisibility

Let's Learn!

A number is **divisible** by another number if you can divide without getting a remainder. For example, think about the equation 32 ÷ 8 = 4. Since there is no remainder, 32 is **divisible** by 8!

Circle the numbers that are divisible by 4.　　14　　(28)　　(44)　　49

Circle the numbers that are divisible by 6.　　12　　16　　24　　54

Circle the numbers that are divisible by 7.　　17　　23　　28　　42

Circle the numbers that are divisible by 9.　　29　　36　　45　　72

Circle the numbers that are divisible by 2.　　546　　251　　722　　863

Challenge yourself! Write a number that would make each statement true.

20 and 45 are both divisible by _____.

12 and 27 are both divisible by _____.

21 and 49 are both divisible by _____.

IXL.com
skill ID
UTK

Let's Learn!

Factors are numbers you multiply together to get another number.

For example, let's find the factors of 15. Think about all of the whole numbers you can multiply together to get 15.

$$1 \times 15 = 15 \qquad 3 \times 5 = 15$$

So the factors of 15 are 1, 3, 5, and 15!

Write all of the factors of each number.

12: _____1, 2, 3, 4, 6, 12_____

9: _____

13: _____

18: _____

24: _____

22: _____

20: _____

23: _____

27: _____

49: _____

IXL.com
skill ID
2S9

Let's Learn!

When you multiply a factor by a whole number, the answer is a **multiple** of that factor.

To find the multiples of a number, multiply that number by 1, 2, 3, and so on. For example, the first four multiples of 5 are 5, 10, 15, and 20.

Write the first four multiples of each number.

4: _____ 4, 8, 12, 16 _____   6: _____

7: _____   9: _____

10: _____   12: _____

15: _____   30: _____

80: _____   112: _____

205: _____

IXL.com
skill ID
ENC

Find the path from start to finish! Step only on spaces with true statements. No diagonal moves are allowed.

START ⬇ FINISH ⬆

6 is a factor of 18.	6 is a multiple of 18.	32 is divisible by 6.	21 is divisible by 7.	14 is a multiple of 2.
27 is a multiple of 3.	24 is divisible by 5.	4 is a factor of 40.	5 is a factor of 30.	4 is a multiple of 12.
16 is a multiple of 2.	35 is a factor of 7.	48 is divisible by 8.	6 is a multiple of 12.	9 is a factor of 24.
20 is divisible by 5.	7 is a factor of 28.	36 is a multiple of 9.	8 is divisible by 32.	18 is a multiple of 4.

Let's Learn!

A **prime** number has only two factors, 1 and itself. For example, 13 is a prime number. Its only factors are 1 and 13.

A **composite** number is not prime. It has at least one factor other than 1 and itself. For example, 10 is a composite number. It has the factors 1, 2, 5, and 10.

The number 1 is neither prime nor composite.

Write all of the factors of each number. Then decide whether the number is prime or composite.

6: _____1, 2, 3, 6_____   Prime   (Composite)

11: _____   Prime   Composite

4: _____   Prime   Composite

16: _____   Prime   Composite

19: _____   Prime   Composite

35: _____   Prime   Composite

23: _____   Prime   Composite

IXL.com
skill ID
TNF

Exploration Zone

PRIME NUMBERS

Follow the steps to find all prime numbers less than 60. The first two steps have been completed for you.

- List all numbers greater than 1 up to 60.

- Since 2 is the smallest prime number, circle it. Then, cross out all numbers that are multiples of 2.

- Move to the next number that has not already been crossed out. (This will be the number 3.) Circle it, and then cross out all numbers that are multiples of 3.

- Repeat until you get to the end of the list. All the circled numbers are prime numbers!

IXL.com
skill ID
L9R

(2)   3   4̷   5   6̷   7   8̷   9   1̷0̷

11   1̷2̷   13   1̷4̷   15   1̷6̷   17   1̷8̷   19   2̷0̷

21   2̷2̷   23   2̷4̷   25   2̷6̷   27   2̷8̷   29   3̷0̷

31   3̷2̷   33   3̷4̷   35   3̷6̷   37   3̷8̷   39   4̷0̷

41   4̷2̷   43   4̷4̷   45   4̷6̷   47   4̷8̷   49   5̷0̷

51   5̷2̷   53   5̷4̷   55   5̷6̷   57   5̷8̷   59   6̷0̷

GOLDBACH'S CONJECTURE

Many mathematicians think prime numbers are interesting. For example, the mathematician Christian Goldbach looked at prime numbers and came up with these rules.

- Every even number greater than 2 can be written as the sum of two prime numbers. For example, 10 = 7 + 3.

- Every odd number greater than 5 can be written as the sum of three prime numbers. For example, 13 = 3 + 5 + 5.

The rules are called Goldbach's conjecture. A **conjecture** is a statement that hasn't been proven. So, nobody knows whether these rules are always true.

TRY IT YOURSELF!

Write these even numbers as the sum of two prime numbers. Use the numbers you circled on the last page to help!

6 = _____ 3 + 3 _____   18 = _____

32 = _____   40 = _____

Write these odd numbers as the sum of three prime numbers. Use the numbers you circled on the last page to help!

17 = _____   33 = _____

41 = _____   59 = _____

Let's Learn!

A **sequence** is a list of numbers that follows a pattern. You can use addition and subtraction to make a sequence. For example, look at the addition sequence below.

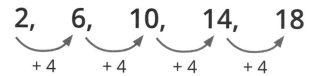

$$2, \quad 6, \quad 10, \quad 14, \quad 18$$

+ 4   + 4   + 4   + 4

To get from one number to the next, you have to add 4. So, the rule for this sequence is to add 4!

Find the next two numbers in each sequence.

Rule: add 75	225	300	375	450	525

Rule: subtract 100	745	645	545		

Rule: add 250	2,340	2,590	2,840		

Rule: subtract 400	5,934	5,534	5,134		

Rule: add 720	7,026	7,746	8,466		

Find the rule and the next two numbers in each sequence.

| Rule: ADD 45 | 577 | 622 | 667 | 712 | 757 |

| Rule: | 1,150 | 1,035 | 920 | | |

| Rule: | 2,075 | 1,715 | 1,355 | | |

| Rule: | 3,040 | 3,500 | 3,960 | | |

| Rule: | 8,900 | 8,380 | 7,860 | | |

Some number sequences use multiplication or division. Find the next two numbers in each sequence.

Rule: multiply by 3	6	18	54	162	486

Rule: divide by 2	192	96	48		

Rule: multiply by 5	6	30	150		

Rule: divide by 7	4,802	686	98		

Rule: multiply by 6	6	36	216		

Rule: divide by 4	2,048	512	128		

Draw lines to match each sequence to its rule.

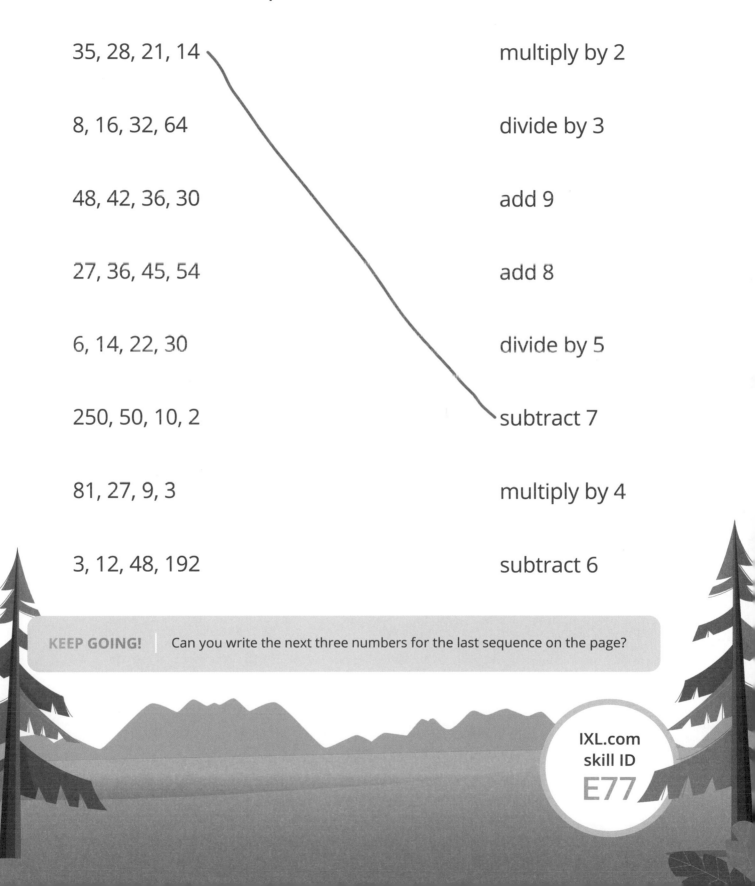

35, 28, 21, 14	multiply by 2
8, 16, 32, 64	divide by 3
48, 42, 36, 30	add 9
27, 36, 45, 54	add 8
6, 14, 22, 30	divide by 5
250, 50, 10, 2	subtract 7
81, 27, 9, 3	multiply by 4
3, 12, 48, 192	subtract 6

KEEP GOING! | Can you write the next three numbers for the last sequence on the page?

Exploration Zone

PATTERNS WITH SHAPES

Sometimes, patterns are represented with shapes. Look at the pattern below.
See how the pattern changes from one figure to the next.

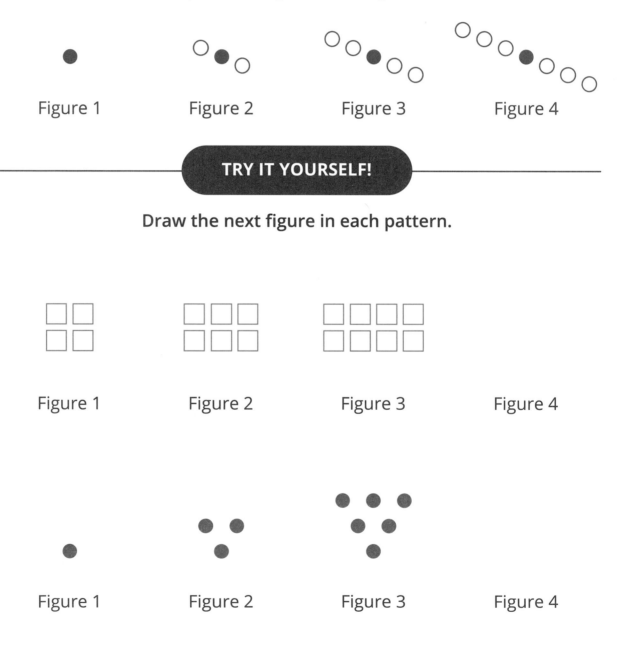

Figure 1 Figure 2 Figure 3 Figure 4

TRY IT YOURSELF!

Draw the next figure in each pattern.

Figure 1 Figure 2 Figure 3 Figure 4

Figure 1 Figure 2 Figure 3 Figure 4

Record the pattern in each table. See if you can finish the
number pattern without drawing!

Figure 1

Figure 2

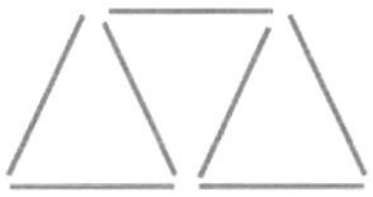

Figure 3

Figure 4

Figure	Number of lines
1	3
2	
3	
4	
5	
6	

Figure 1

Figure 2

Figure 3

Figure 4

Figure	Number of squares
1	
2	
3	
4	
5	
6	

FIBONACCI SEQUENCE

One of the most famous number patterns is the Fibonacci sequence. In the sequence, the number being added follows its own pattern. See if you can unlock the secret of the Fibonacci sequence!

What do you notice? How would you describe the Fibonacci sequence?

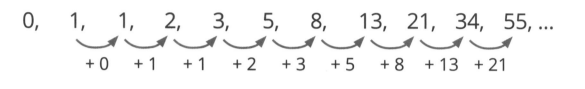

0, 1, 1, 2, 3, 5, 8, 13, 21, 34, 55, ...

+ 0 + 1 + 1 + 2 + 3 + 5 + 8 + 13 + 21

TRY IT YOURSELF!

Use what you noticed about the Fibonacci sequence to write the next six numbers in the sequence.

_____, _____, _____, _____, _____, _____

You can use numbers to represent whole amounts. For example, here is 1 pie.

But what if you have only part of a pie? You can use a **fraction** to describe this amount. Here is $\frac{5}{6}$ of a pie.

$\frac{5}{6}$ ← The **numerator** tells the number of parts you have.
← The **denominator** tells the number of equal parts in the whole.

Write the fraction shown.

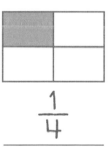

$\frac{1}{4}$

_____

_____

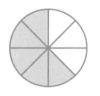

_____

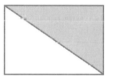

_____

_____

For more practice, visit IXL.com or the IXL mobile app and enter this code in the search bar.

IXL.com skill ID

YHL

Let's Learn!

You can also use fractions to represent parts of a set. For example, $\frac{3}{4}$ of these donuts have sprinkles.

$\frac{3}{4}$ ← 3 donuts with sprinkles
← 4 donuts in all

Answer each question.

What fraction of the fruit are oranges?

$\frac{3}{5}$

_____

What fraction of the drinks have straws?

_____

What fraction of the bugs are bees?

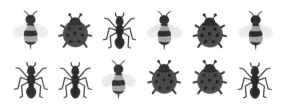

_____

What fraction of the animals are pigs?

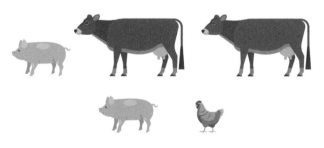

_____

Let's Learn!

You can show fractions on number lines. This number line shows $\frac{2}{7}$.

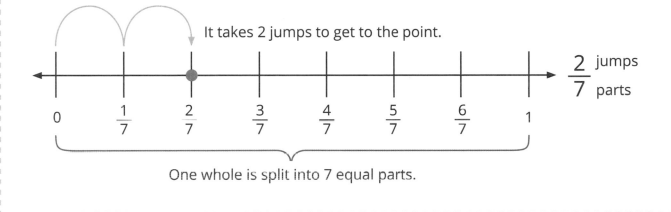

It takes 2 jumps to get to the point.

$\frac{2}{7}$ jumps
   parts

0    $\frac{1}{7}$ $\frac{2}{7}$ $\frac{3}{7}$ $\frac{4}{7}$ $\frac{5}{7}$ $\frac{6}{7}$ 1

One whole is split into 7 equal parts.

Label the number line. Write the fraction shown.

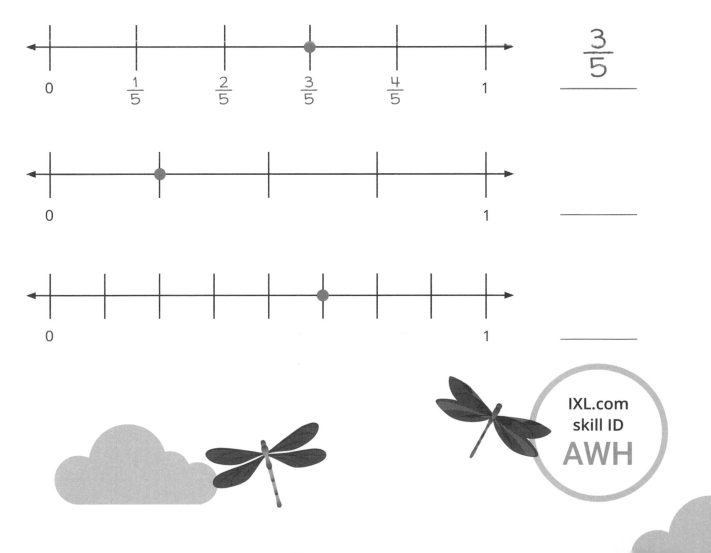

0    $\frac{1}{5}$ $\frac{2}{5}$ $\frac{3}{5}$ $\frac{4}{5}$ 1 $\frac{3}{5}$

0   1   _____

0   1   _____

Draw each fraction.

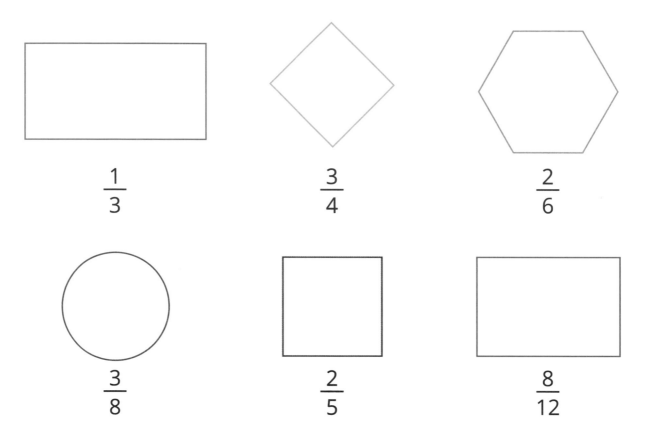

$$\frac{1}{3}$$

$$\frac{3}{4}$$

$$\frac{2}{6}$$

$$\frac{3}{8}$$

$$\frac{2}{5}$$

$$\frac{8}{12}$$

Shade in each fraction.

$$\frac{1}{2}$$

$$\frac{2}{3}$$

$$\frac{5}{7}$$

$$\frac{3}{5}$$

$$\frac{1}{4}$$

$$\frac{5}{6}$$

Modeling fractions

Show each fraction on the number line.

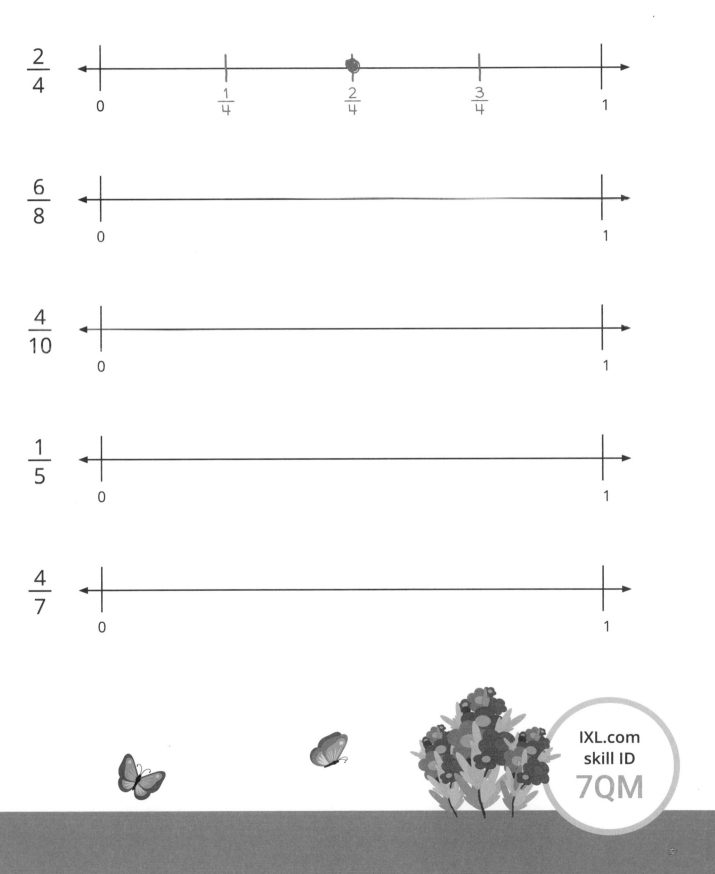

$\dfrac{2}{4}$

0     $\dfrac{1}{4}$ $\dfrac{2}{4}$ $\dfrac{3}{4}$ 1

$\dfrac{6}{8}$ 0 — 1

$\dfrac{4}{10}$ 0 — 1

$\dfrac{1}{5}$ 0 — 1

$\dfrac{4}{7}$ 0 — 1

IXL.com skill ID

7QM

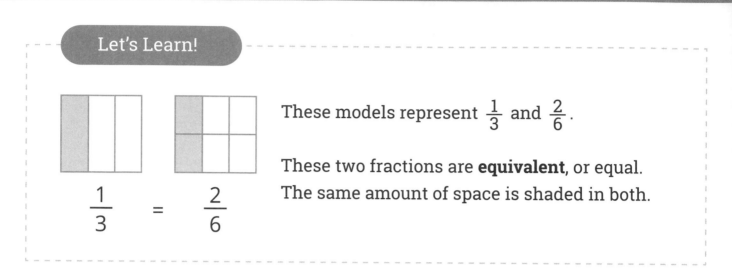

Let's Learn!

These models represent $\frac{1}{3}$ and $\frac{2}{6}$.

These two fractions are **equivalent**, or equal.
The same amount of space is shaded in both.

$$\frac{1}{3} = \frac{2}{6}$$

Shade in the equivalent fraction. Write the new fraction.

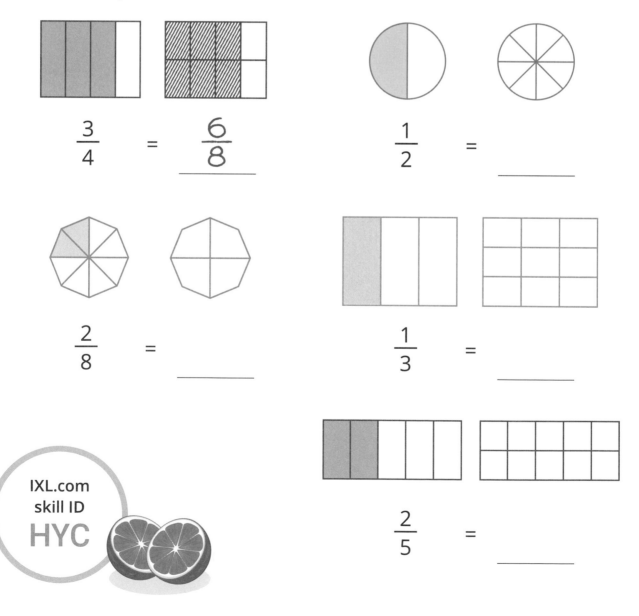

$$\frac{3}{4} = \frac{6}{8}$$

$$\frac{1}{2} = \underline{\hspace{2cm}}$$

$$\frac{2}{8} = \underline{\hspace{2cm}}$$

$$\frac{1}{3} = \underline{\hspace{2cm}}$$

$$\frac{2}{5} = \underline{\hspace{2cm}}$$

IXL.com
skill ID
HYC

Show the equivalent fraction on the number line. Write the new fraction.

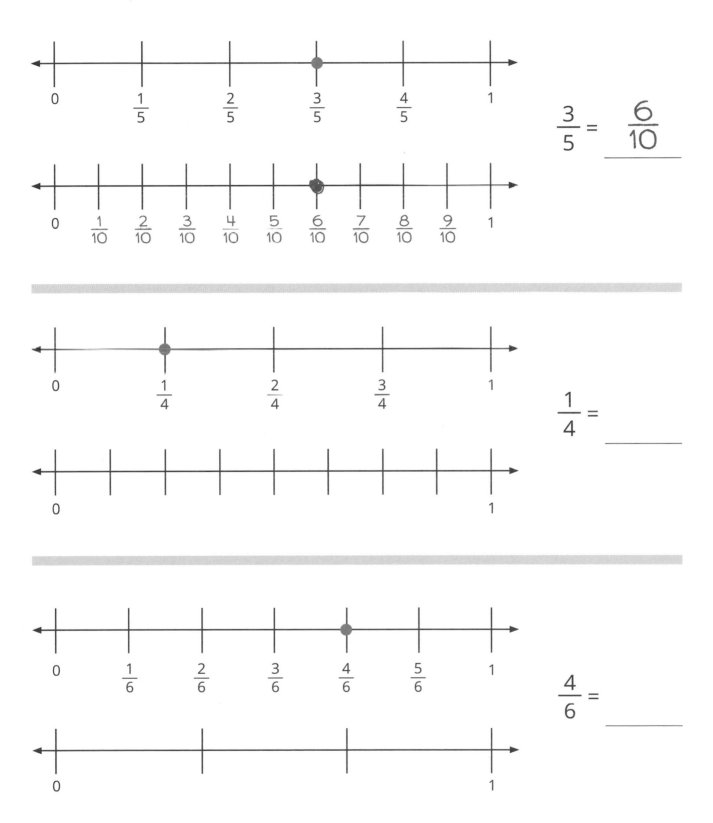

$$\frac{3}{5} = \frac{6}{10}$$

$$\frac{1}{4} =$$ _____

$$\frac{4}{6} =$$ _____

Let's Learn!

If you multiply the top and bottom of a fraction by the same number, you will get an equivalent fraction.

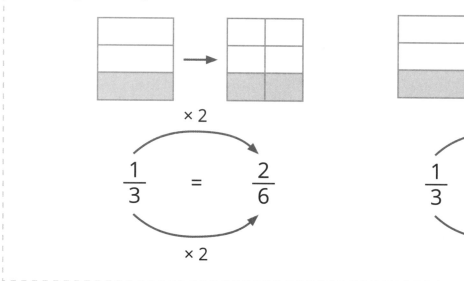

$$\frac{1}{3} = \frac{2}{6} \qquad \frac{1}{3} = \frac{3}{9}$$

Make equivalent fractions.

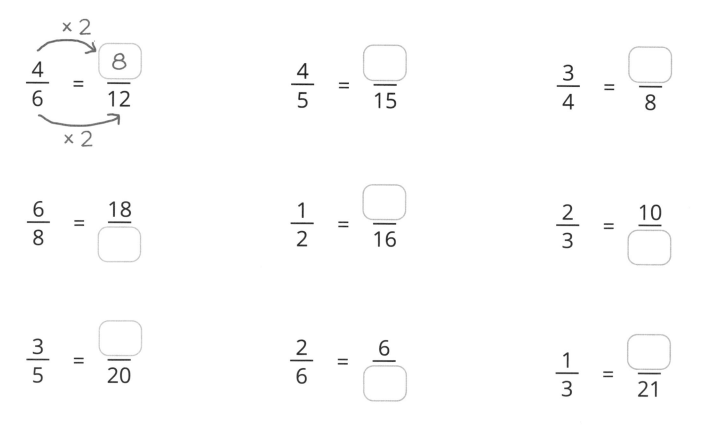

$$\frac{4}{6} = \frac{8}{12}$$

$$\frac{4}{5} = \frac{\square}{15}$$

$$\frac{3}{4} = \frac{\square}{8}$$

$$\frac{6}{8} = \frac{18}{\square}$$

$$\frac{1}{2} = \frac{\square}{16}$$

$$\frac{2}{3} = \frac{10}{\square}$$

$$\frac{3}{5} = \frac{\square}{20}$$

$$\frac{2}{6} = \frac{6}{\square}$$

$$\frac{1}{3} = \frac{\square}{21}$$

Let's Learn!

You can divide the top and bottom of a fraction by the same number to get an equivalent fraction, too. You will want to divide by a number that is a **factor** of both the numerator and the denominator.

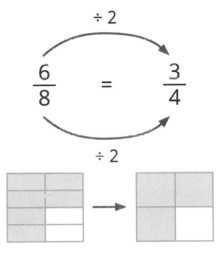

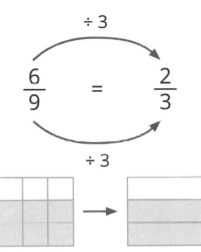

Make equivalent fractions.

$$\frac{3}{9} = \frac{1}{3} \quad (\div 3)$$

$$\frac{6}{10} = \frac{\boxed{}}{5}$$

$$\frac{8}{12} = \frac{2}{\boxed{}}$$

$$\frac{9}{12} = \frac{3}{\boxed{}}$$

$$\frac{4}{16} = \frac{\boxed{}}{4}$$

$$\frac{3}{15} = \frac{1}{\boxed{}}$$

$$\frac{8}{20} = \frac{2}{\boxed{}}$$

$$\frac{15}{25} = \frac{3}{\boxed{}}$$

IXL.com
skill ID
7CY

Let's Learn!

To find the simplest form of a fraction, divide the top and bottom by the common factors until you can't anymore.

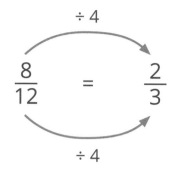

For example, the simplest form of $\frac{8}{12}$ is $\frac{2}{3}$.

Write each fraction in simplest form.

$\frac{12}{16} = \frac{3}{4}$

$\frac{4}{10} = $ _____

$\frac{10}{15} = $ _____

$\frac{6}{9} = $ _____

$\frac{4}{14} = $ _____

$\frac{12}{20} = $ _____

$\frac{20}{24} = $ _____

$\frac{14}{28} = $ _____

IXL.com
skill ID
3R5

Tell whether each fraction is in simplest form. If not, write it in simplest form.

$\dfrac{4}{8}$ _____ NO, $\dfrac{1}{2}$ _____

$\dfrac{4}{5}$ _____ YES _____

$\dfrac{6}{18}$ _____

$\dfrac{10}{24}$ _____

$\dfrac{2}{3}$ _____

$\dfrac{10}{20}$ _____

$\dfrac{8}{32}$ _____

$\dfrac{7}{10}$ _____

$\dfrac{6}{11}$ _____

$\dfrac{16}{40}$ _____

$\dfrac{9}{45}$ _____

$\dfrac{18}{27}$ _____

Let's Learn!

When two fractions have the same denominator, they have the same number of total parts. You can compare the numerators to see which fraction is bigger.

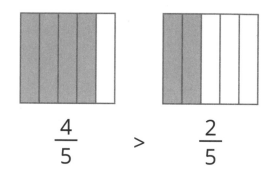

$$\frac{4}{5} \quad > \quad \frac{2}{5}$$

Compare each pair of fractions. Fill in each circle with > , <, or =.

$$\frac{3}{4} \enspace \fbox{>} \enspace \frac{2}{4} \qquad\qquad\qquad \frac{1}{3} \bigcirc \frac{2}{3}$$

$$\frac{5}{6} \bigcirc \frac{4}{6} \qquad\qquad\qquad \frac{7}{12} \bigcirc \frac{6}{12}$$

$$\frac{5}{8} \bigcirc \frac{3}{8} \qquad\qquad\qquad \frac{8}{9} \bigcirc \frac{8}{9}$$

$$\frac{4}{10} \bigcirc \frac{8}{10} \qquad\qquad\qquad \frac{1}{7} \bigcirc \frac{3}{7}$$

Let's Learn!

A **unit fraction** is a fraction with a numerator of 1. You can compare unit fractions by looking at the denominators. The larger the denominator, the smaller the fraction.

$\frac{1}{2}$ $\frac{1}{4}$ $\frac{1}{6}$

Write each fraction. Fill in each circle with > , <, or =.

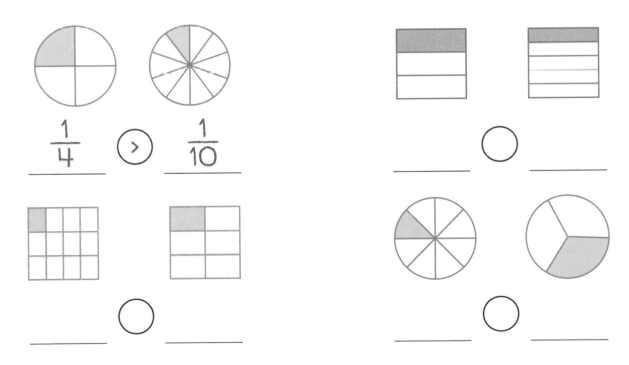

$\frac{1}{4}$ ⟩ $\frac{1}{10}$

Compare each pair of fractions. Fill in each circle with > , <, or =.

$\frac{1}{5}$ ◯ $\frac{1}{6}$ $\frac{1}{7}$ ◯ $\frac{1}{9}$ $\frac{1}{8}$ ◯ $\frac{1}{2}$

IXL.com
skill ID
Q87

> **Let's Learn!**
>
> You can use the rule for comparing unit fractions to compare other fractions, too.
>
> For example, think about $\frac{3}{4}$ and $\frac{3}{8}$. They have the same number of shaded parts, but fourths are bigger than eighths. So, $\frac{3}{4}$ must be greater than $\frac{3}{8}$.
>
> $\frac{3}{4}$ > $\frac{3}{8}$

Compare each pair of fractions. Fill in each circle with > , <, or =.

$\frac{5}{8}$ ⃝> $\frac{5}{10}$ $\frac{2}{3}$ ◯ $\frac{2}{5}$

$\frac{4}{9}$ ◯ $\frac{4}{6}$ $\frac{7}{8}$ ◯ $\frac{7}{12}$

$\frac{6}{12}$ ◯ $\frac{6}{12}$ $\frac{3}{5}$ ◯ $\frac{3}{4}$

Keep going! Fill in each circle with >, <, or =. Think about how big the pieces are and how many are shaded.

$\frac{2}{7}$ ◯ $\frac{4}{5}$ $\frac{4}{6}$ ◯ $\frac{3}{10}$ $\frac{3}{4}$ ◯ $\frac{2}{5}$

Compare each pair of fractions. Fill in each circle with > , <, or =.

$\frac{4}{5}$ ◯ $\frac{3}{5}$ $\frac{1}{9}$ ◯ $\frac{1}{5}$ $\frac{3}{6}$ ◯ $\frac{3}{8}$

$\frac{1}{4}$ ◯ $\frac{1}{3}$ $\frac{6}{8}$ ◯ $\frac{7}{8}$ $\frac{4}{5}$ ◯ $\frac{4}{8}$

$\frac{10}{11}$ ◯ $\frac{10}{12}$ $\frac{3}{12}$ ◯ $\frac{2}{12}$ $\frac{7}{9}$ ◯ $\frac{8}{9}$

$\frac{14}{15}$ ◯ $\frac{13}{15}$ $\frac{12}{16}$ ◯ $\frac{12}{15}$ $\frac{20}{25}$ ◯ $\frac{20}{30}$

Let's Learn!

The fraction $\frac{1}{2}$ is called a **benchmark fraction**. Benchmark fractions are easy to see on a number line. Notice that $\frac{1}{2}$ is easy to see because it is exactly halfway between 0 and 1.

You can compare any fraction to a benchmark. For example, compare $\frac{1}{2}$ and $\frac{3}{4}$. The fraction $\frac{3}{4}$ is farther right on the number line than $\frac{1}{2}$.

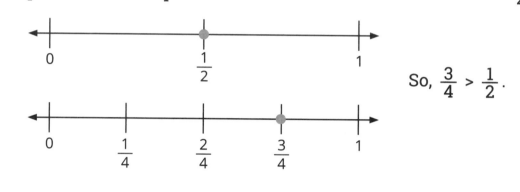

So, $\frac{3}{4} > \frac{1}{2}$.

Compare each fraction to $\frac{1}{2}$. Fill in each circle with >, <, or =.

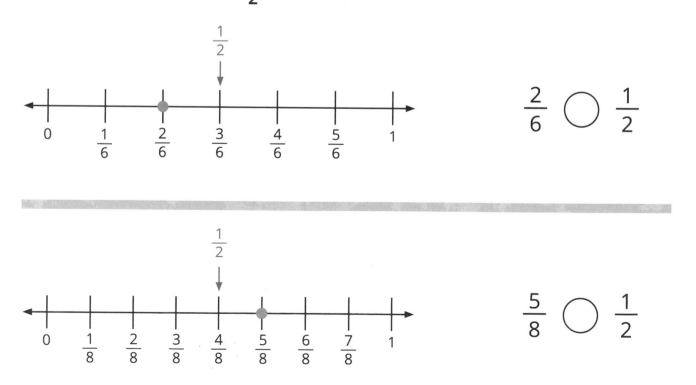

$\frac{2}{6} \bigcirc \frac{1}{2}$

$\frac{5}{8} \bigcirc \frac{1}{2}$

Compare each fraction to $\frac{1}{2}$. Fill in each circle with >, <, or =.

$\frac{2}{8} \bigcirc \frac{1}{2}$ $\frac{5}{6} \bigcirc \frac{1}{2}$ $\frac{4}{5} \bigcirc \frac{1}{2}$

$\frac{2}{4} \bigcirc \frac{1}{2}$ $\frac{1}{6} \bigcirc \frac{1}{2}$ $\frac{7}{10} \bigcirc \frac{1}{2}$

$\frac{3}{8} \bigcirc \frac{1}{2}$ $\frac{6}{12} \bigcirc \frac{1}{2}$ $\frac{4}{9} \bigcirc \frac{1}{2}$

$\frac{2}{5} \bigcirc \frac{1}{2}$ $\frac{4}{7} \bigcirc \frac{1}{2}$ $\frac{4}{8} \bigcirc \frac{1}{2}$

Let's Learn!

You can use benchmark fractions such as $\frac{1}{2}$ to compare other fractions. Let's try it for $\frac{4}{6}$ and $\frac{3}{8}$.

First, compare each fraction to $\frac{1}{2}$. You know that $\frac{4}{6} > \frac{1}{2}$ and $\frac{3}{8} < \frac{1}{2}$. So, $\frac{4}{6}$ must be greater than $\frac{3}{8}$!

Use $\frac{1}{2}$ as a benchmark to compare each pair of fractions. Fill in each circle with >, <, or =.

$\frac{1}{3} \bigcirc \frac{3}{4}$ $\frac{7}{12} \bigcirc \frac{2}{5}$ $\frac{2}{6} \bigcirc \frac{8}{10}$

$\frac{2}{8} \bigcirc \frac{3}{5}$ $\frac{3}{8} \bigcirc \frac{4}{7}$ $\frac{5}{10} \bigcirc \frac{3}{6}$

$\frac{2}{6} \bigcirc \frac{4}{8}$ $\frac{2}{3} \bigcirc \frac{4}{12}$ $\frac{5}{11} \bigcirc \frac{7}{8}$

$\frac{4}{7} \bigcirc \frac{2}{6}$ $\frac{5}{10} \bigcirc \frac{6}{9}$ $\frac{1}{3} \bigcirc \frac{3}{5}$

IXL.com
skill ID
EHJ

You can use equivalent fractions to make comparing fractions easier. If you start with fractions with different denominators, try finding equivalent fractions that have the same denominator.

Write equivalent fractions to compare each pair of fractions. Fill in each circle with >, <, or =.

$\dfrac{9}{12} \; \dfrac{3}{4} \; \bigcirc{>} \; \dfrac{7}{12}$

$\dfrac{1}{5} \; \bigcirc \; \dfrac{3}{10}$

$\dfrac{2}{3} \; \bigcirc \; \dfrac{5}{9}$

$\dfrac{5}{8} \; \bigcirc \; \dfrac{3}{4}$

$\dfrac{4}{6} \; \bigcirc \; \dfrac{2}{3}$

$\dfrac{1}{3} \; \bigcirc \; \dfrac{5}{12}$

$\dfrac{1}{3} \; \bigcirc \; \dfrac{2}{9}$

$\dfrac{3}{4} \; \bigcirc \; \dfrac{8}{12}$

Let's Learn!

The Least Common Multiple (LCM) of two numbers is the smallest multiple that two numbers have in common. Let's try it for a couple of examples.

Multiples of 2: 2, 4, 6, 8, 10, 12...

Multiples of 3: 3, 6, 9, 12, 15...

The LCM of 2 and 3 is 6!

Multiples of 4: 4, 8, 12, 16, 20, 24, 28...

Multiples of 6: 6, 12, 18, 24, 30...

The LCM of 4 and 6 is 12!

You can use the LCM to help compare fractions.

Find the LCM of each pair of numbers. Then use the LCM to make equivalent fractions. Fill in each circle with >, <, or =.

LCM of 3 and 4: ___12___

$$\frac{8}{12} \; \frac{2}{3} \; \bigcirc< \; \frac{3}{4} \; \frac{9}{12}$$

LCM of 3 and 7: _____

$$\frac{1}{3} \; \bigcirc \; \frac{2}{7}$$

LCM of 9 and 6: _____

$$\frac{7}{9} \; \bigcirc \; \frac{4}{6}$$

LCM of 3 and 6: _____

$$\frac{2}{3} \; \bigcirc \; \frac{5}{6}$$

Find the LCM of each pair of numbers. Then use the LCM to make equivalent fractions. Fill in each circle with >, <, or =.

LCM of 4 and 6: _____

$\dfrac{1}{4}$ ◯ $\dfrac{2}{6}$

LCM of 3 and 8: _____

$\dfrac{2}{3}$ ◯ $\dfrac{6}{8}$

LCM of 4 and 10: _____

$\dfrac{3}{10}$ ◯ $\dfrac{1}{4}$

LCM of 5 and 7: _____

$\dfrac{2}{5}$ ◯ $\dfrac{3}{7}$

LCM of 4 and 7: _____

$\dfrac{3}{4}$ ◯ $\dfrac{5}{7}$

LCM of 12 and 9: _____

$\dfrac{8}{12}$ ◯ $\dfrac{6}{9}$

LCM of 8 and 10: _____

$\dfrac{2}{8}$ ◯ $\dfrac{3}{10}$

LCM of 8 and 12: _____

$\dfrac{5}{8}$ ◯ $\dfrac{7}{12}$

IXL.com
skill ID
R7P

Compare the fractions. Fill in each circle with >, <, or =.

$\frac{3}{4}$ ◯ $\frac{5}{8}$ $\frac{2}{5}$ ◯ $\frac{3}{10}$ $\frac{2}{6}$ ◯ $\frac{1}{3}$

$\frac{2}{6}$ ◯ $\frac{5}{12}$ $\frac{4}{9}$ ◯ $\frac{1}{3}$ $\frac{1}{3}$ ◯ $\frac{3}{12}$

$\frac{1}{4}$ ◯ $\frac{3}{12}$ $\frac{2}{8}$ ◯ $\frac{1}{3}$ $\frac{3}{4}$ ◯ $\frac{4}{6}$

$\frac{7}{10}$ ◯ $\frac{3}{4}$ $\frac{5}{7}$ ◯ $\frac{2}{3}$ $\frac{3}{5}$ ◯ $\frac{4}{6}$

Challenge yourself! Write a number to make each statement true.

$\frac{5}{8}$ > $\frac{3}{\boxed{}}$ $\frac{4}{5}$ > $\frac{6}{\boxed{}}$ $\frac{2}{5}$ < $\frac{\boxed{}}{8}$

Write the fractions in order from least to greatest.

$\frac{2}{3}$ $\frac{1}{5}$ $\frac{1}{3}$ $\frac{1}{5}$ $\frac{1}{3}$ $\frac{2}{3}$

$\frac{6}{10}$ $\frac{4}{5}$ $\frac{4}{10}$ _____ _____ _____

$\frac{5}{6}$ $\frac{2}{5}$ $\frac{2}{12}$ _____ _____ _____

$\frac{2}{5}$ $\frac{3}{10}$ $\frac{1}{4}$ _____ _____ _____

$\frac{3}{4}$ $\frac{2}{3}$ $\frac{5}{6}$ _____ _____ _____

Challenge yourself! Write the fractions in order from least to greatest.

$\frac{3}{4}$ $\frac{5}{8}$ $\frac{1}{2}$ $\frac{4}{12}$ _____ _____ _____ _____

$\frac{2}{3}$ $\frac{5}{12}$ $\frac{2}{6}$ $\frac{1}{4}$ _____ _____ _____ _____

Answer each question.

According to the weather forecast, $\frac{2}{3}$ of a foot of snow was supposed to fall last night. Jackson measured the snow this morning and found that $\frac{3}{4}$ of a foot had fallen. Was that more or less than the weather forecast?

_____

Evan lives $\frac{5}{6}$ of a mile from the library and $\frac{8}{12}$ of a mile from the post office. Does Evan live closer to the library or the post office?

_____

Robin and Kristi are painting their fingernails. They decide to paint some fingernails purple and some fingernails blue. Robin paints $\frac{4}{5}$ of her fingernails purple. Kristi paints $\frac{7}{10}$ of her fingernails purple. Who painted more of her fingernails purple?

_____

Dylan takes his dog to the dog park. Dylan notices that $\frac{2}{5}$ of the dogs at the dog park have red leashes and $\frac{1}{4}$ of the dogs have blue leashes. Do more of the dogs at the dog park have red leashes or blue leashes?

_____

Annie cut two pieces of yarn to make a key chain. The blue piece is $\frac{5}{8}$ of a foot. The orange piece is $\frac{2}{3}$ of a foot. Which piece of yarn is shorter?

_____

You can add unit fractions to make other fractions.

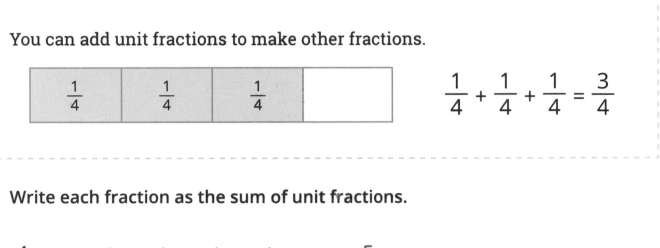

Write each fraction as the sum of unit fractions.

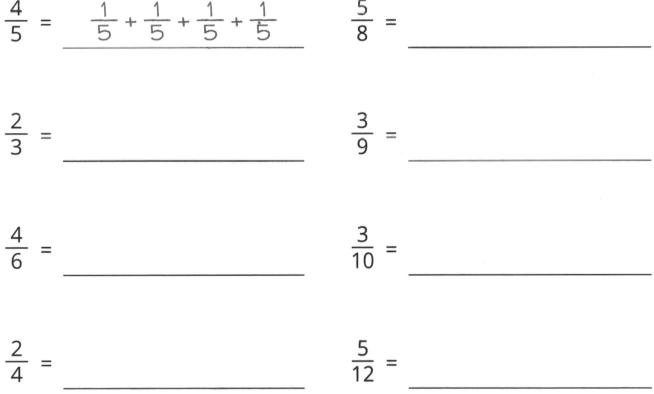

$$\frac{4}{5} = \frac{1}{5} + \frac{1}{5} + \frac{1}{5} + \frac{1}{5}$$

$$\frac{5}{8} = $$

$$\frac{2}{3} = $$

$$\frac{3}{9} = $$

$$\frac{4}{6} = $$

$$\frac{3}{10} = $$

$$\frac{2}{4} = $$

$$\frac{5}{12} = $$

Let's Learn!

You can add larger fractions, too. Look at the pictures to see how!

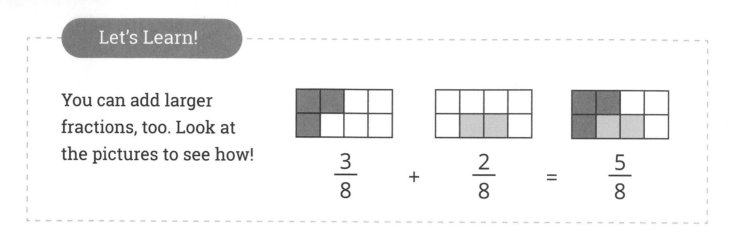

$$\frac{3}{8} \quad + \quad \frac{2}{8} \quad = \quad \frac{5}{8}$$

Add. Shade in the missing fraction.

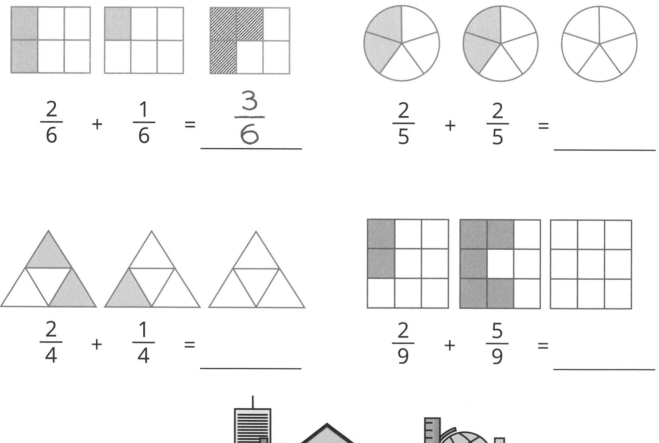

$$\frac{2}{6} \quad + \quad \frac{1}{6} \quad = \quad \frac{3}{6}$$

$$\frac{2}{5} \quad + \quad \frac{2}{5} \quad = \quad \rule{2cm}{0.4pt}$$

$$\frac{2}{4} \quad + \quad \frac{1}{4} \quad = \quad \rule{2cm}{0.4pt}$$

$$\frac{2}{9} \quad + \quad \frac{5}{9} \quad = \quad \rule{2cm}{0.4pt}$$

Let's Learn!

To add fractions with the same denominator, add the numerators. The denominator stays the same.

$$\frac{1}{9} + \frac{4}{9} = \frac{5}{9}$$

Add.

$$\frac{2}{8} + \frac{3}{8} = \underline{\hspace{2cm}}$$

$$\frac{1}{4} + \frac{2}{4} = \underline{\hspace{2cm}}$$

$$\frac{1}{5} + \frac{3}{5} = \underline{\hspace{2cm}}$$

$$\frac{4}{8} + \frac{3}{8} = \underline{\hspace{2cm}}$$

$$\frac{5}{9} + \frac{3}{9} = \underline{\hspace{2cm}}$$

$$\frac{1}{6} + \frac{4}{6} = \underline{\hspace{2cm}}$$

$$\frac{4}{10} + \frac{4}{10} = \underline{\hspace{2cm}}$$

$$\frac{3}{7} + \frac{2}{7} = \underline{\hspace{2cm}}$$

$$\frac{4}{11} + \frac{5}{11} = \underline{\hspace{2cm}}$$

$$\frac{1}{5} + \frac{2}{5} = \underline{\hspace{2cm}}$$

$$\frac{7}{12} + \frac{4}{12} = \underline{\hspace{2cm}}$$

IXL.com
skill ID
PDU

Let's Learn!

You can subtract fractions, too! Look at the pictures to see how.

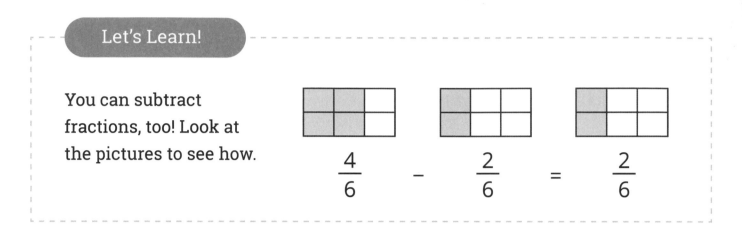

$$\frac{4}{6} - \frac{2}{6} = \frac{2}{6}$$

Subtract. Shade in the missing fraction.

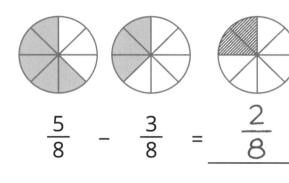

$$\frac{5}{8} - \frac{3}{8} = \frac{2}{8}$$

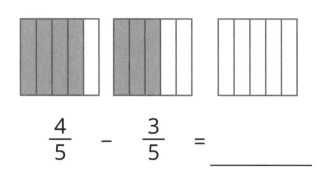

$$\frac{4}{5} - \frac{3}{5} = \underline{\qquad}$$

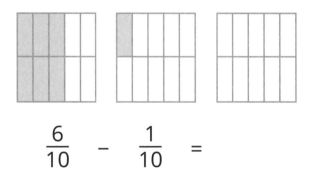

$$\frac{6}{10} - \frac{1}{10} = \underline{\qquad}$$

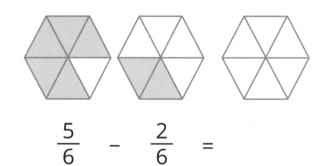

$$\frac{5}{6} - \frac{2}{6} = \underline{\qquad}$$

Let's Learn!

To subtract fractions with the same denominator, subtract the numerators. The denominator stays the same.

$$\frac{9}{10} - \frac{5}{10} = \frac{4}{10}$$

Subtract.

$$\frac{2}{3} - \frac{1}{3} = \underline{\hspace{2cm}}$$

$$\frac{6}{8} - \frac{2}{8} = \underline{\hspace{2cm}}$$

$$\frac{4}{5} - \frac{2}{5} = \underline{\hspace{2cm}}$$

$$\frac{3}{4} - \frac{2}{4} = \underline{\hspace{2cm}}$$

$$\frac{3}{6} - \frac{1}{6} = \underline{\hspace{2cm}}$$

$$\frac{8}{10} - \frac{3}{10} = \underline{\hspace{2cm}}$$

$$\frac{4}{7} - \frac{2}{7} = \underline{\hspace{2cm}}$$

$$\frac{7}{9} - \frac{2}{9} = \underline{\hspace{2cm}}$$

$$\frac{10}{12} - \frac{4}{12} = \underline{\hspace{2cm}}$$

$$\frac{4}{8} - \frac{1}{8} = \underline{\hspace{2cm}}$$

$$\frac{9}{11} - \frac{2}{11} = \underline{\hspace{2cm}}$$

IXL.com
skill ID
AVF

Add or subtract.

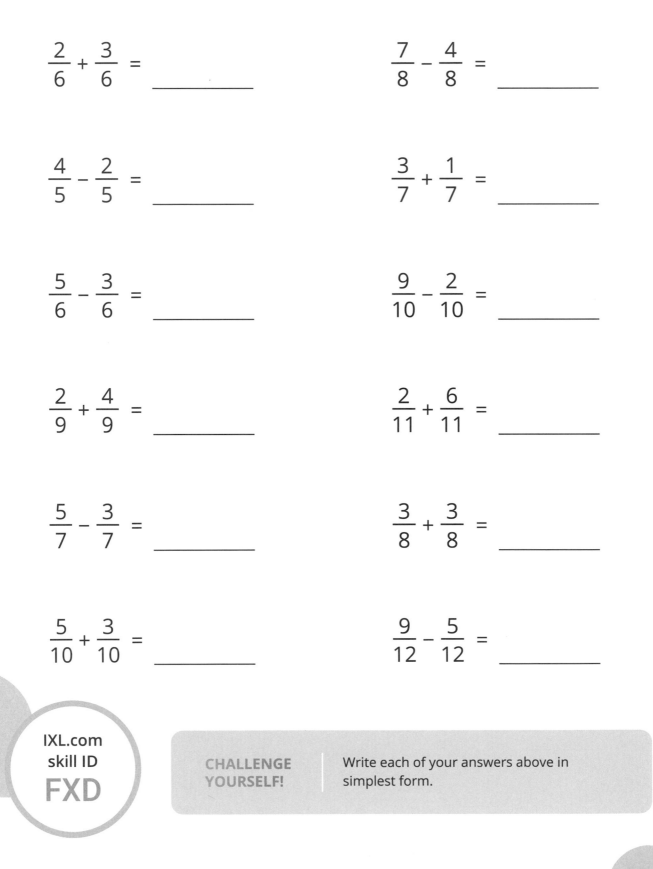

$$\frac{2}{6} + \frac{3}{6} = \underline{\hspace{2cm}}$$

$$\frac{7}{8} - \frac{4}{8} = \underline{\hspace{2cm}}$$

$$\frac{4}{5} - \frac{2}{5} = \underline{\hspace{2cm}}$$

$$\frac{3}{7} + \frac{1}{7} = \underline{\hspace{2cm}}$$

$$\frac{5}{6} - \frac{3}{6} = \underline{\hspace{2cm}}$$

$$\frac{9}{10} - \frac{2}{10} = \underline{\hspace{2cm}}$$

$$\frac{2}{9} + \frac{4}{9} = \underline{\hspace{2cm}}$$

$$\frac{2}{11} + \frac{6}{11} = \underline{\hspace{2cm}}$$

$$\frac{5}{7} - \frac{3}{7} = \underline{\hspace{2cm}}$$

$$\frac{3}{8} + \frac{3}{8} = \underline{\hspace{2cm}}$$

$$\frac{5}{10} + \frac{3}{10} = \underline{\hspace{2cm}}$$

$$\frac{9}{12} - \frac{5}{12} = \underline{\hspace{2cm}}$$

IXL.com
skill ID

FXD

CHALLENGE YOURSELF! Write each of your answers above in simplest form.

Answer each question.

Joseph bought a quart of vanilla ice cream. He used $\frac{3}{8}$ of a quart for a sundae. He then used $\frac{1}{8}$ of a quart for a root beer float. How much more ice cream did Joseph use in the sundae than in the root beer float?

_____

Zoey is at a hot-air balloon festival with her family. She notices that $\frac{4}{12}$ of the balloons are yellow and $\frac{3}{12}$ of the balloons are green. What fraction of the hot-air balloons are yellow or green?

_____

Mona shared a large pizza with her brother. Mona ate $\frac{2}{8}$ of the pizza, and her brother ate $\frac{3}{8}$ of the pizza. What fraction of the pizza did they eat altogether?

_____

Juan and his brother are using cornstarch in two science experiments. They use $\frac{2}{4}$ of a cup of cornstarch to make an exploding volcano. Then they use $\frac{1}{4}$ of a cup of cornstarch to make magic ooze. What fraction of a cup do they use in all?

_____

At the beginning of the month, Camille's bottle of scented lotion was $\frac{4}{5}$ full. By the end of the month, it was $\frac{2}{5}$ full. What fraction of the bottle did Camille use this month?

_____

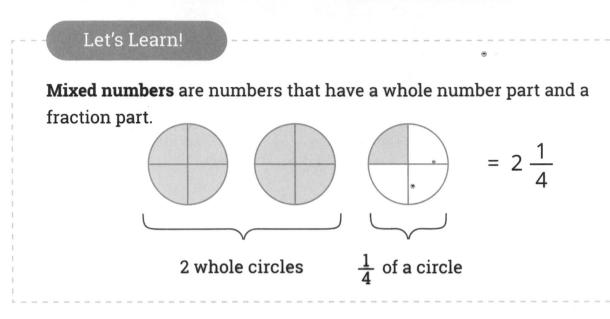

Let's Learn!

Mixed numbers are numbers that have a whole number part and a fraction part.

$= 2\frac{1}{4}$

2 whole circles $\frac{1}{4}$ of a circle

Write the mixed number shown.

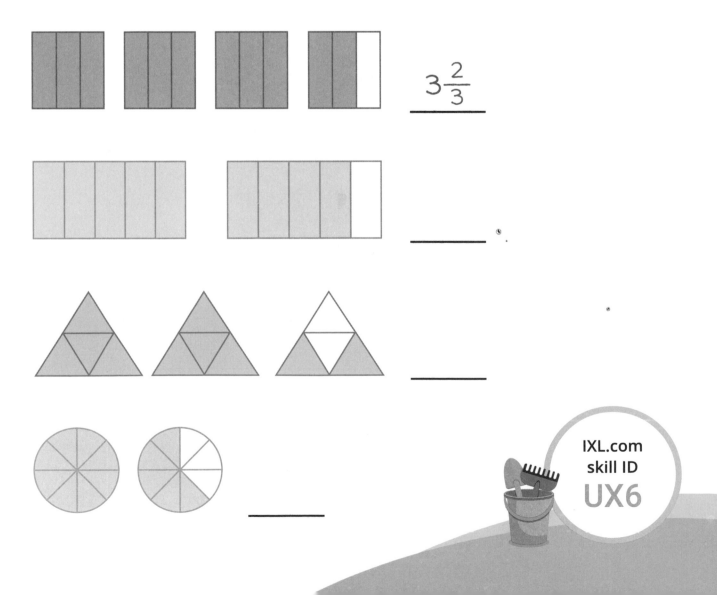

$3\frac{2}{3}$

_____

_____

_____

_____

IXL.com
skill ID
UX6

Make a model to show each mixed number.

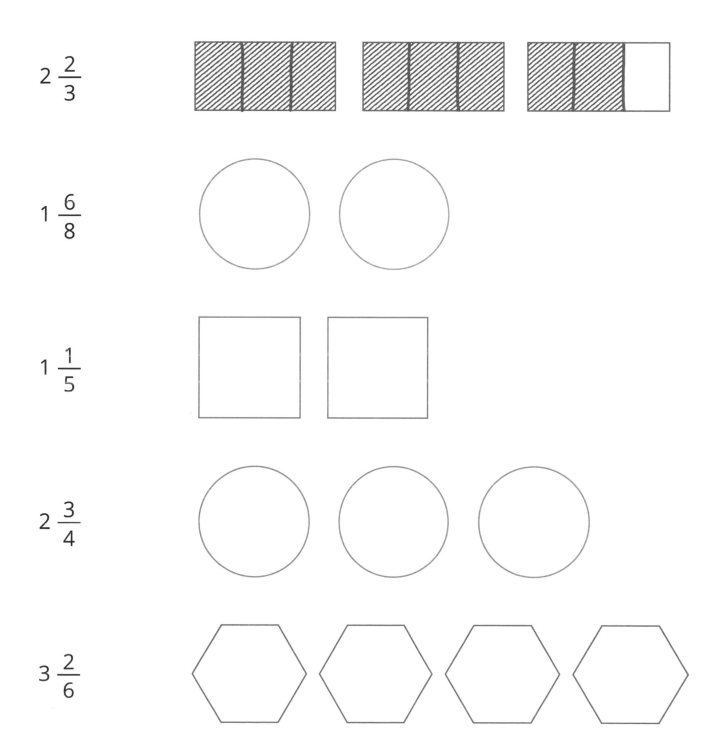

$2\dfrac{2}{3}$

$1\dfrac{6}{8}$

$1\dfrac{1}{5}$

$2\dfrac{3}{4}$

$3\dfrac{2}{6}$

Let's Learn!

You can also use an **improper fraction** to show fractions that are greater than one. Improper fractions are fractions whose numerators are larger than their denominators.

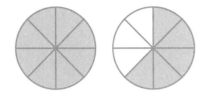

$\dfrac{13}{8}$ ← number of shaded parts

← number of equal parts per whole

Write each improper fraction shown.

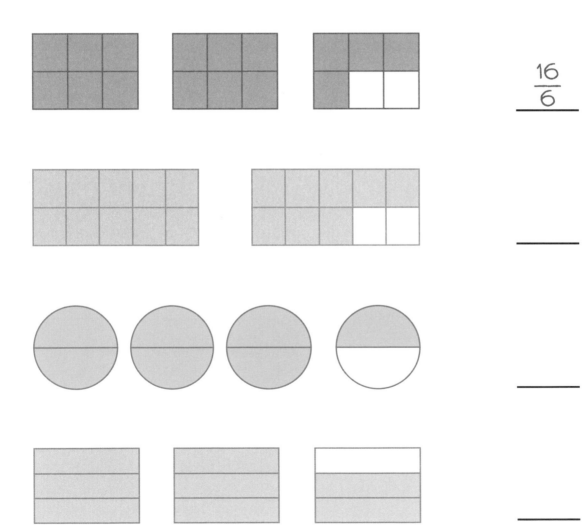

$\dfrac{16}{6}$

_____

_____

_____

Make a model to show each improper fraction.

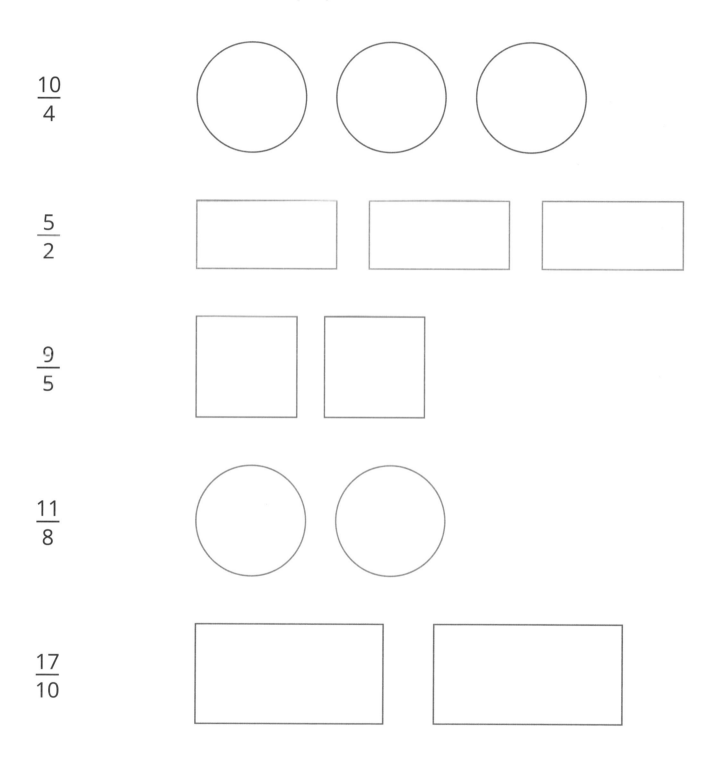

$\dfrac{10}{4}$

$\dfrac{5}{2}$

$\dfrac{9}{5}$

$\dfrac{11}{8}$

$\dfrac{17}{10}$

Let's Learn!

You can write improper fractions as mixed numbers or whole numbers to represent the same amount.

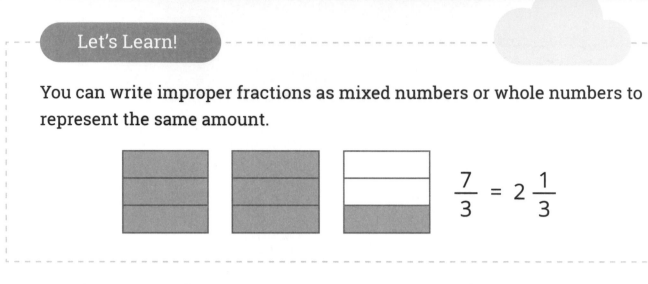

$$\frac{7}{3} = 2\frac{1}{3}$$

Write each improper fraction as a mixed number or a whole number.

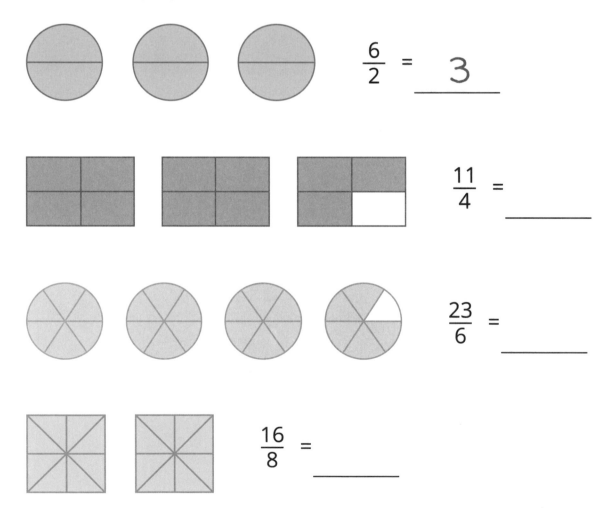

$$\frac{6}{2} = \underline{}3\underline{}$$

$$\frac{11}{4} = \underline{}$$

$$\frac{23}{6} = \underline{}$$

$$\frac{16}{8} = \underline{}$$

Write each improper fraction as a mixed number or a whole number.

$\dfrac{11}{3}$ = $3\dfrac{2}{3}$ _____ $\dfrac{7}{4}$ = _____

$\dfrac{14}{6}$ = _____ $\dfrac{27}{9}$ = _____

$\dfrac{17}{12}$ = _____ $\dfrac{25}{8}$ = _____

Write each mixed number as an improper fraction.

$2\dfrac{2}{5}$ = $\dfrac{12}{5}$ _____ $2\dfrac{3}{8}$ = _____

$4\dfrac{1}{2}$ = _____ $2\dfrac{3}{7}$ = _____

$3\dfrac{3}{10}$ = _____ $3\dfrac{5}{11}$ = _____

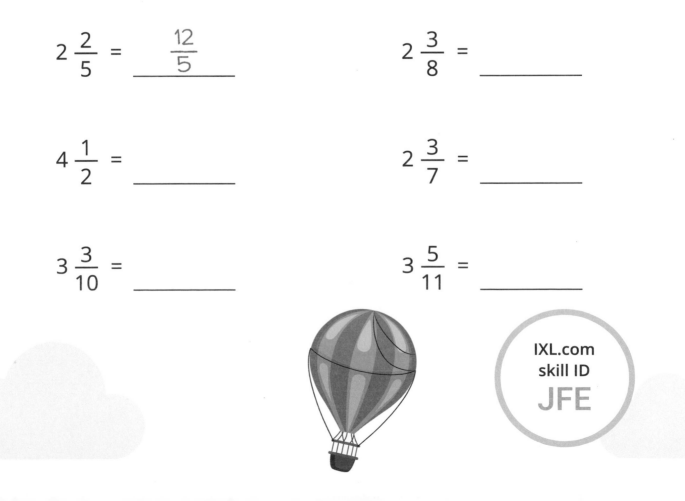

IXL.com
skill ID
JFE

Let's Learn!

You can add mixed numbers by adding the whole number parts and then adding the fraction parts. Try it with $2\frac{1}{4} + 1\frac{2}{4}$.

Add the whole number parts: $2 + 1 = 3$.

Add the fraction parts: $\frac{1}{4} + \frac{2}{4} = \frac{3}{4}$. Then put them together.

$$2\frac{1}{4} \quad + \quad 1\frac{2}{4} \quad = \quad 3\frac{3}{4}$$

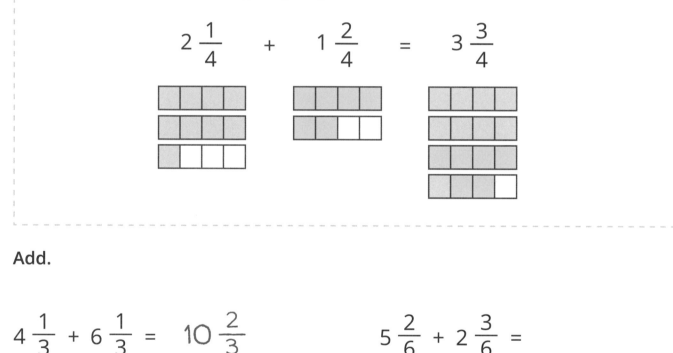

Add.

$4\frac{1}{3} + 6\frac{1}{3} = \underline{10\frac{2}{3}}$

$5\frac{2}{6} + 2\frac{3}{6} = \underline{\hspace{2cm}}$

$7\frac{4}{8} + 3\frac{2}{8} = \underline{\hspace{2cm}}$

$4\frac{3}{9} + 9\frac{4}{9} = \underline{\hspace{2cm}}$

$2\frac{3}{10} + 11\frac{5}{10} = \underline{\hspace{2cm}}$

$13\frac{5}{12} + 5\frac{5}{12} = \underline{\hspace{2cm}}$

Add.

$9\frac{1}{4} + 4\frac{1}{4} =$ _____

$11\frac{3}{7} + 7\frac{1}{7} =$ _____

$8\frac{1}{5} + 8\frac{1}{5} =$ _____

$14\frac{3}{8} + 12\frac{2}{8} =$ _____

$8\frac{2}{9} + 12\frac{5}{9} =$ _____

$22\frac{2}{6} + 6\frac{2}{6} =$ _____

$27\frac{3}{10} + 10\frac{5}{10} =$ _____

$9\frac{2}{12} + 16\frac{7}{12} =$ _____

$24\frac{5}{11} + 19\frac{5}{11} =$ _____

$13\frac{3}{8} + 18\frac{1}{8} =$ _____

Let's Learn!

When you add mixed numbers, the fraction part may become larger than a whole. For example, when you add $3\frac{3}{4} + 1\frac{2}{4}$, you get $4\frac{5}{4}$. Since $\frac{5}{4}$ is larger than a whole, you can regroup.

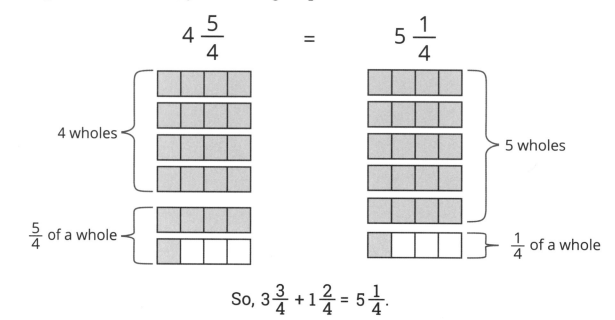

$$4\frac{5}{4} \qquad = \qquad 5\frac{1}{4}$$

4 wholes

$\frac{5}{4}$ of a whole

5 wholes

$\frac{1}{4}$ of a whole

So, $3\frac{3}{4} + 1\frac{2}{4} = 5\frac{1}{4}$.

Add. Regroup the sum.

$4\frac{2}{3} + 2\frac{2}{3} = 6\frac{4}{3} = 7\frac{1}{3}$

$3\frac{3}{5} + 5\frac{4}{5} =$ _____

$6\frac{4}{8} + 3\frac{6}{8} =$ _____

$2\frac{2}{4} + 8\frac{3}{4} =$ _____

$12\frac{6}{9} + 6\frac{5}{9} =$ _____

$10\frac{7}{12} + 7\frac{9}{12} =$ _____

Add. Regroup the sum.

$12 \dfrac{7}{8} + 4 \dfrac{3}{8} =$ _____

$2 \dfrac{9}{10} + 17 \dfrac{7}{10} =$ _____

$13 \dfrac{5}{7} + 13 \dfrac{5}{7} =$ _____

$16 \dfrac{3}{6} + 23 \dfrac{5}{6} =$ _____

$16 \dfrac{4}{5} + 22 \dfrac{4}{5} =$ _____

$21 \dfrac{4}{11} + 14 \dfrac{7}{11} =$ _____

$15 \dfrac{7}{9} + 28 \dfrac{8}{9} =$ _____

$17 \dfrac{8}{12} + 11 \dfrac{8}{12} =$ _____

$23 \dfrac{7}{10} + 7 \dfrac{3}{10} =$ _____

$25 \dfrac{5}{7} + 2 \dfrac{6}{7} =$ _____

$17 \dfrac{9}{11} + 29 \dfrac{5}{11} =$ _____

$37 \dfrac{10}{12} + 17 \dfrac{7}{12} =$ _____

Add. Regroup the sum, if necessary.

$3\dfrac{4}{5} + 3\dfrac{3}{5} = $ _____

$2\dfrac{3}{6} + 4\dfrac{2}{6} = $ _____

$5\dfrac{1}{4} + 7\dfrac{2}{4} = $ _____

$9\dfrac{2}{3} + 3\dfrac{2}{3} = $ _____

$4\dfrac{6}{10} + 4\dfrac{7}{10} = $ _____

$6\dfrac{5}{8} + 7\dfrac{4}{8} = $ _____

$3\dfrac{2}{7} + 10\dfrac{3}{7} = $ _____

$4\dfrac{4}{12} + 3\dfrac{3}{12} = $ _____

$5\dfrac{3}{9} + 5\dfrac{8}{9} = $ _____

$13\dfrac{4}{5} + 4\dfrac{2}{5} = $ _____

Let's Learn!

You can subtract mixed numbers by subtracting the whole number parts and then subtracting the fraction parts. Try it with $3\frac{2}{3} - 1\frac{1}{3}$.

Subtract the whole number parts: $3 - 1 = 2$.

Subtract the fraction parts: $\frac{2}{3} - \frac{1}{3} = \frac{1}{3}$. Then put them together.

$$3\frac{2}{3} - 1\frac{1}{3} = 2\frac{1}{3}$$

Subtract.

$5\frac{2}{3} - 1\frac{1}{3} = \underline{4\frac{1}{3}}$

$8\frac{4}{5} - 5\frac{2}{5} = \underline{\hspace{2cm}}$

$7\frac{7}{8} - 2\frac{3}{8} = \underline{\hspace{2cm}}$

$15\frac{2}{4} - 7\frac{1}{4} = \underline{\hspace{2cm}}$

$16\frac{8}{12} - 8\frac{3}{12} = \underline{\hspace{2cm}}$

$19\frac{7}{9} - 12\frac{3}{9} = \underline{\hspace{2cm}}$

Subtract.

$16 \dfrac{3}{5} - 3 \dfrac{2}{5} =$ _____

$10 \dfrac{3}{8} - 7 \dfrac{1}{8} =$ _____

$12 \dfrac{3}{4} - 6 \dfrac{1}{4} =$ _____

$18 \dfrac{5}{6} - 10 \dfrac{5}{6} =$ _____

$17 \dfrac{5}{12} - 6 \dfrac{3}{12} =$ _____

$19 \dfrac{8}{9} - 12 \dfrac{6}{9} =$ _____

$21 \dfrac{4}{5} - 13 \dfrac{1}{5} =$ _____

$20 \dfrac{5}{7} - 15 \dfrac{3}{7} =$ _____

$27 \dfrac{9}{12} - 8 \dfrac{7}{12} =$ _____

$15 \dfrac{5}{8} - 14 \dfrac{4}{8} =$ _____

Let's Learn!

Sometimes when you subtract mixed numbers, the first fraction part is smaller than the second fraction part, and you can't subtract them. For example, with $3\frac{1}{3} - 1\frac{2}{3}$, you can't subtract $\frac{1}{3} - \frac{2}{3}$.

So, regroup! You can rewrite $3\frac{1}{3}$ as $2\frac{4}{3}$.

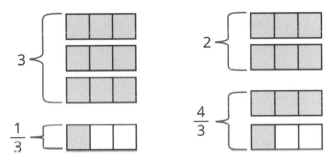

Rewrite the problem and solve.

$$2\frac{4}{3} - 1\frac{2}{3} = 1\frac{2}{3}$$

Subtract.

$7\frac{11}{8}\ 8\frac{\cancel{3}}{8} - 3\frac{5}{8} = \underline{4\frac{6}{8}}$ $5\frac{3}{6} - 2\frac{5}{6} = \underline{\qquad}$

$7\frac{2}{5} - 5\frac{4}{5} = \underline{\qquad}$ $14\frac{4}{9} - 8\frac{7}{9} = \underline{\qquad}$

Keep going! Subtract.

$6 \frac{8}{8} \cancel{7} - 3 \frac{7}{8} = \underline{\quad 3 \frac{1}{8} \quad}$

$8 \frac{1}{4} - 1 \frac{3}{4} = \underline{\qquad}$

$11 \frac{4}{6} - 2 \frac{5}{6} = \underline{\qquad}$

$15 \frac{2}{10} - 12 \frac{7}{10} = \underline{\qquad}$

$16 - 6 \frac{5}{8} = \underline{\qquad}$

$19 \frac{7}{12} - 10 \frac{9}{12} = \underline{\qquad}$

$12 \frac{3}{9} - 7 \frac{8}{9} = \underline{\qquad}$

$10 \frac{1}{7} - 4 \frac{2}{7} = \underline{\qquad}$

$17 \frac{6}{11} - 3 \frac{10}{11} = \underline{\qquad}$

$24 - 19 \frac{5}{6} = \underline{\qquad}$

$27 \frac{2}{12} - 18 \frac{6}{12} = \underline{\qquad}$

$15 \frac{4}{9} - 7 \frac{7}{9} = \underline{\qquad}$

Subtract. Regroup, if necessary.

$10\frac{1}{5} - 4\frac{3}{5} = $ _____

$5\frac{1}{4} - 1\frac{3}{4} = $ _____

$6\frac{5}{6} - 2\frac{3}{6} = $ _____

$8\frac{4}{5} - 4\frac{2}{5} = $ _____

$10\frac{3}{9} - 4\frac{5}{9} = $ _____

$12\frac{7}{12} - 7\frac{4}{12} = $ _____

$9 - 2\frac{4}{6} = $ _____

$15\frac{4}{10} - 7\frac{5}{10} = $ _____

$18\frac{3}{7} - 12\frac{1}{7} = $ _____

$13 - 9\frac{2}{3} = $ _____

Add or subtract. Regroup, if necessary.

$10 \frac{5}{8} - 6 \frac{4}{8} =$ _____

$13 \frac{5}{6} + 12 \frac{5}{6} =$ _____

$19 \frac{2}{9} + 11 \frac{5}{9} =$ _____

$8 \frac{2}{5} - 7 \frac{3}{5} =$ _____

$5 \frac{5}{7} + 16 \frac{2}{7} =$ _____

$14 \frac{9}{12} + 6 \frac{1}{12} =$ _____

$9 \frac{8}{9} - 2 \frac{4}{9} =$ _____

$14 \frac{5}{10} - 8 \frac{9}{10} =$ _____

$19 \frac{7}{11} + 17 \frac{9}{11} =$ _____

$13 - 8 \frac{1}{4} =$ _____

IXL.com
skill ID
9AS

$25 \frac{4}{7} + 15 \frac{6}{7} =$ _____

Answer each question.

On a field trip to Riverview Orchard, Ms. Miller's class picked $7\frac{2}{8}$ pounds of strawberries and $4\frac{7}{8}$ pounds of blueberries. How many pounds of berries did they pick in all?

_____

Paco is $5\frac{3}{12}$ feet tall. His younger brother is $3\frac{5}{12}$ feet tall. In feet, how much taller is Paco than his younger brother?

_____

The cook at the Lazyriver Diner used $12\frac{1}{4}$ cups of flour to make pancakes and $8\frac{3}{4}$ cups of flour to make waffles. How much flour did the cook use in all?

_____

On Saturday, Xavier played basketball with his friends for $2\frac{1}{3}$ hours. On Sunday, he played basketball for $1\frac{2}{3}$ hours. How much longer did Xavier play basketball on Saturday than on Sunday?

_____

Mr. Johnson planned a park clean-up event. He ordered 12 pizzas for the volunteers to eat when they finished cleaning. There were $1\frac{2}{8}$ pizzas left when the event ended. How much pizza did the volunteers eat?

_____

IXL.com
skill ID

6KM

Let's Learn!

You can multiply fractions by whole numbers. Think about repeated addition to help. For example, when you multiply $3 \times \frac{2}{7}$, you are adding $\frac{2}{7}$ three times.

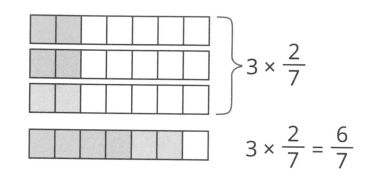

$3 \times \frac{2}{7}$

$3 \times \frac{2}{7} = \frac{6}{7}$

Multiply.

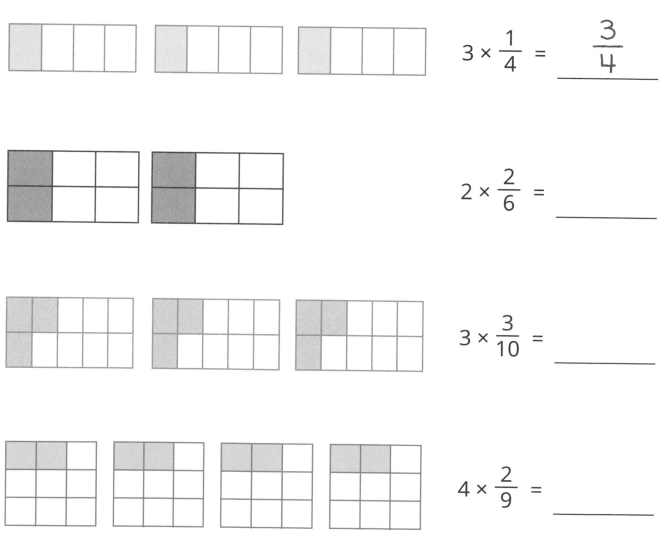

$3 \times \frac{1}{4} = \dfrac{3}{4}$

$2 \times \frac{2}{6} = $ _____

$3 \times \frac{3}{10} = $ _____

$4 \times \frac{2}{9} = $ _____

Multiply.

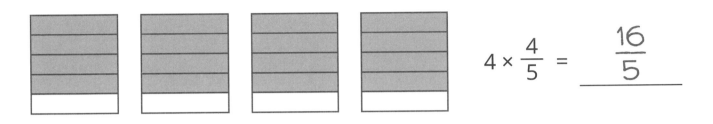

$$4 \times \frac{4}{5} = \frac{16}{5}$$

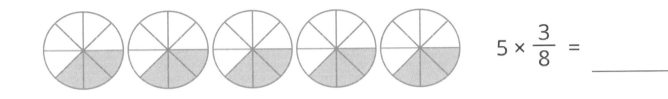

$$5 \times \frac{3}{8} = \underline{\hspace{2cm}}$$

$$3 \times \frac{2}{4} = \underline{\hspace{2cm}}$$

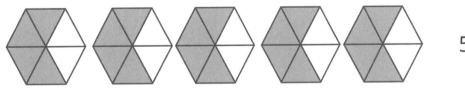

$$5 \times \frac{4}{6} = \underline{\hspace{2cm}}$$

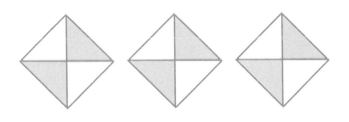

$$2 \times \frac{2}{3} = \underline{\hspace{2cm}}$$

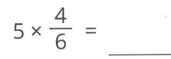

IXL.com
skill ID
Y5C

Write the multiplication equation for each model.

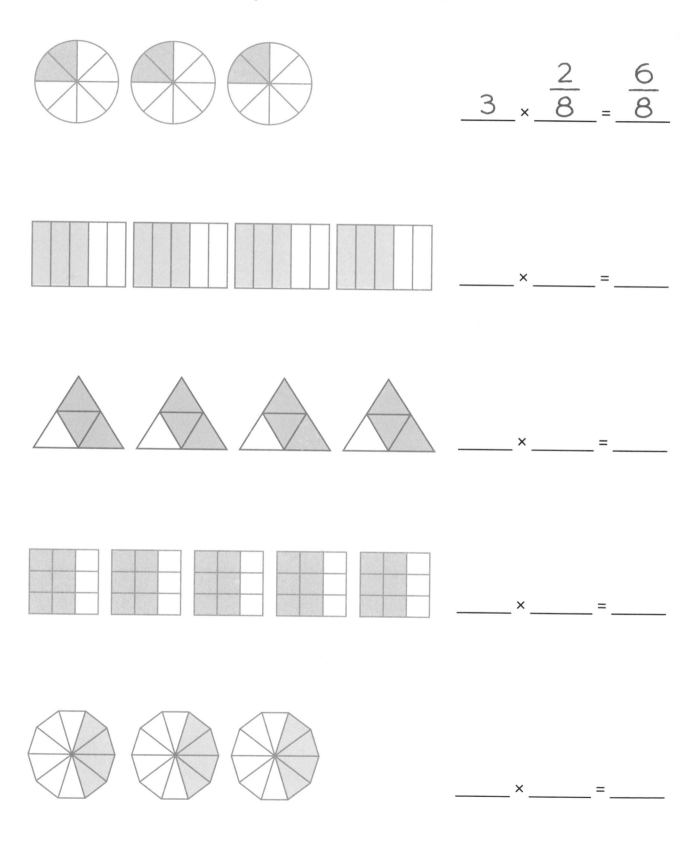

$$\underline{3} \times \underline{\dfrac{2}{8}} = \underline{\dfrac{6}{8}}$$

$$\underline{} \times \underline{} = \underline{}$$

$$\underline{} \times \underline{} = \underline{}$$

$$\underline{} \times \underline{} = \underline{}$$

$$\underline{} \times \underline{} = \underline{}$$

Let's Learn!

To multiply a fraction by a whole number, multiply the numerator by the whole number. Keep the denominator the same.

$$6 \times \frac{2}{5} = \frac{6 \times 2}{5} = \frac{12}{5}$$

Multiply.

$6 \times \dfrac{3}{5} =$ _____

$4 \times \dfrac{2}{8} =$ _____

$7 \times \dfrac{1}{4} =$ _____

$3 \times \dfrac{4}{5} =$ _____

$6 \times \dfrac{2}{11} =$ _____

$8 \times \dfrac{4}{9} =$ _____

$9 \times \dfrac{3}{10} =$ _____

$7 \times \dfrac{3}{7} =$ _____

$7 \times \dfrac{4}{6} =$ _____

$11 \times \dfrac{2}{10} =$ _____

Multiply.

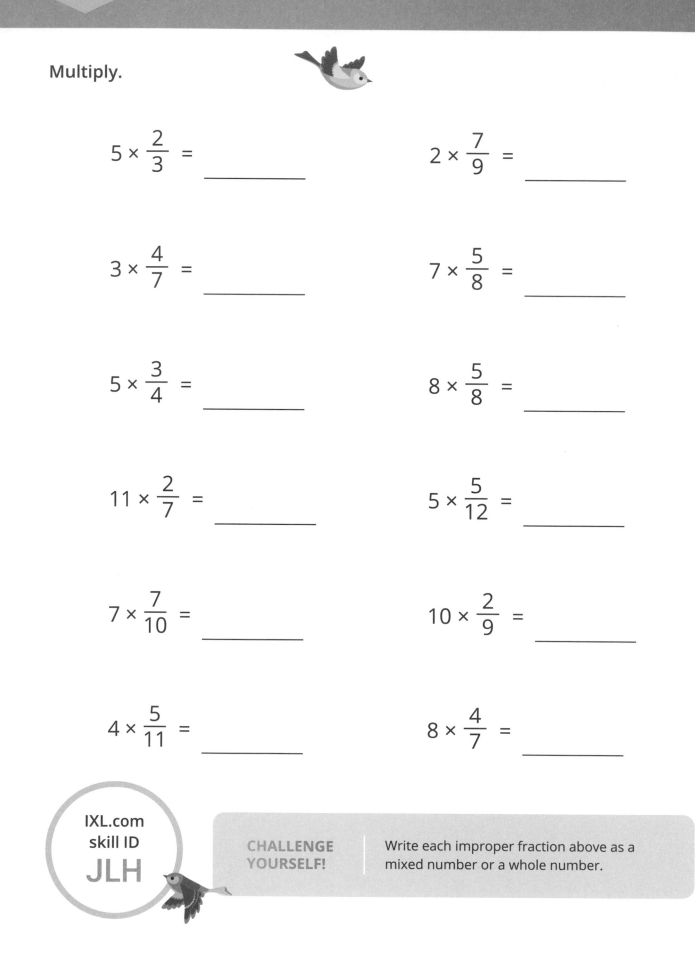

$5 \times \dfrac{2}{3} =$ _____

$2 \times \dfrac{7}{9} =$ _____

$3 \times \dfrac{4}{7} =$ _____

$7 \times \dfrac{5}{8} =$ _____

$5 \times \dfrac{3}{4} =$ _____

$8 \times \dfrac{5}{8} =$ _____

$11 \times \dfrac{2}{7} =$ _____

$5 \times \dfrac{5}{12} =$ _____

$7 \times \dfrac{7}{10} =$ _____

$10 \times \dfrac{2}{9} =$ _____

$4 \times \dfrac{5}{11} =$ _____

$8 \times \dfrac{4}{7} =$ _____

IXL.com
skill ID
JLH

CHALLENGE YOURSELF! | Write each improper fraction above as a mixed number or a whole number.

Multiply. Compare the answers using >, <, or =.

$4 \times \dfrac{4}{5}$ $\boxed{>}$ $6 \times \dfrac{2}{5}$

$\dfrac{16}{5}$ $>$ $\dfrac{12}{5}$

$2 \times \dfrac{3}{4}$ $\bigcirc$ $3 \times \dfrac{1}{4}$

$7 \times \dfrac{4}{6}$ $\bigcirc$ $5 \times \dfrac{5}{6}$

$3 \times \dfrac{3}{8}$ $\bigcirc$ $5 \times \dfrac{6}{8}$

$6 \times \dfrac{3}{10}$ $\bigcirc$ $3 \times \dfrac{6}{10}$

$7 \times \dfrac{5}{7}$ $\bigcirc$ $4 \times \dfrac{8}{7}$

$8 \times \dfrac{7}{9}$ $\bigcirc$ $6 \times \dfrac{8}{9}$

$9 \times \dfrac{8}{12}$ $\bigcirc$ $7 \times \dfrac{6}{12}$

Answer each question. If your answer is greater than 1, write your answer as a mixed number.

Madison is making bags of slime for her friends. She will need $\frac{1}{8}$ of a cup of glue for each bag of slime. How many cups of glue will she need to make 5 bags of slime?

_____

Zion and Alex tried out for the swim team. Zion swam $\frac{1}{5}$ of a mile. Alex swam 3 times as far as Zion. How far did Alex swim?

_____

Diego feeds his dog $\frac{3}{4}$ of a cup of dog food 2 times a day. How many cups of dog food does Diego feed to his dog each day?

_____

At Scoops Ice Cream Shop, there is a sprinkle machine. If you press the button once, you get $\frac{1}{2}$ of a tablespoon of sprinkles. If Harrison presses the button 4 times, how many tablespoons of sprinkles will he get?

_____

IXL.com
skill ID
LX8

Add, subtract, or multiply. Regroup, if necessary.

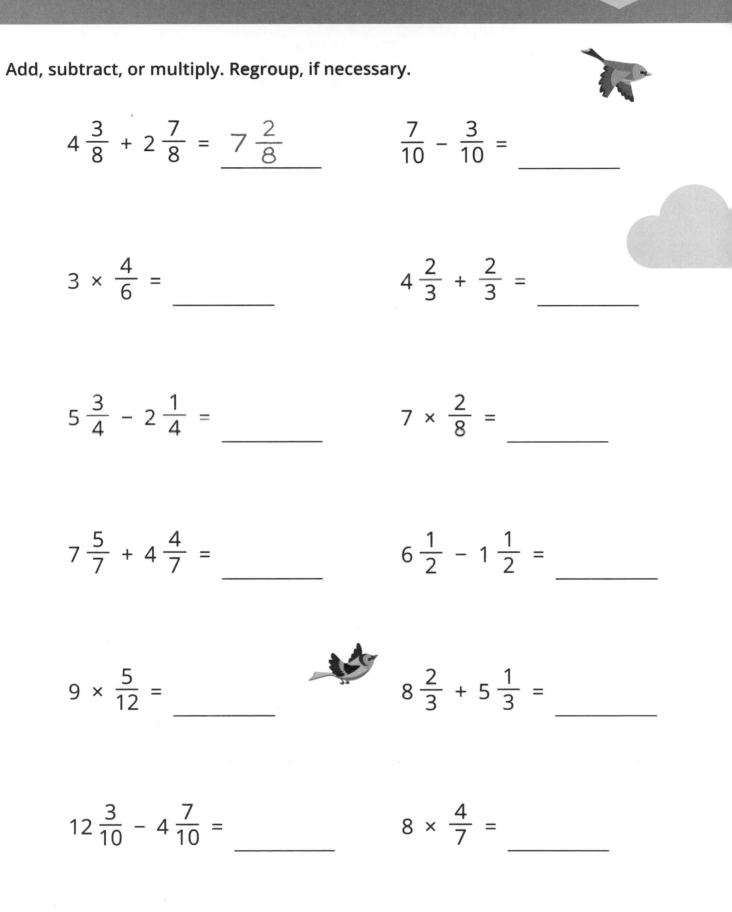

$4\dfrac{3}{8} + 2\dfrac{7}{8} =$ $7\dfrac{2}{8}$ _____

$\dfrac{7}{10} - \dfrac{3}{10} =$ _____

$3 \times \dfrac{4}{6} =$ _____

$4\dfrac{2}{3} + \dfrac{2}{3} =$ _____

$5\dfrac{3}{4} - 2\dfrac{1}{4} =$ _____

$7 \times \dfrac{2}{8} =$ _____

$7\dfrac{5}{7} + 4\dfrac{4}{7} =$ _____

$6\dfrac{1}{2} - 1\dfrac{1}{2} =$ _____

$9 \times \dfrac{5}{12} =$ _____

$8\dfrac{2}{3} + 5\dfrac{1}{3} =$ _____

$12\dfrac{3}{10} - 4\dfrac{7}{10} =$ _____

$8 \times \dfrac{4}{7} =$ _____

Add, subtract, or multiply. Regroup, if necessary.

$9 \times \dfrac{9}{10} =$ _____

$4\dfrac{2}{3} + 6\dfrac{1}{3} =$ _____

$18\dfrac{3}{5} - 2\dfrac{2}{5} =$ _____

$8 \times \dfrac{8}{9} =$ _____

$13\dfrac{1}{7} - 10\dfrac{5}{7} =$ _____

$17\dfrac{4}{6} + 11\dfrac{4}{6} =$ _____

$14\dfrac{5}{9} - 7\dfrac{6}{9} =$ _____

$10 \times \dfrac{7}{8} =$ _____

$13\dfrac{7}{11} + 9\dfrac{9}{11} =$ _____

$4 \times \dfrac{9}{12} =$ _____

$19\dfrac{3}{8} - 6\dfrac{5}{8} =$ _____

$18\dfrac{5}{7} + 23\dfrac{4}{7} =$ _____

Willow and her mom are making homemade granola. This recipe shows the ingredients they will use.

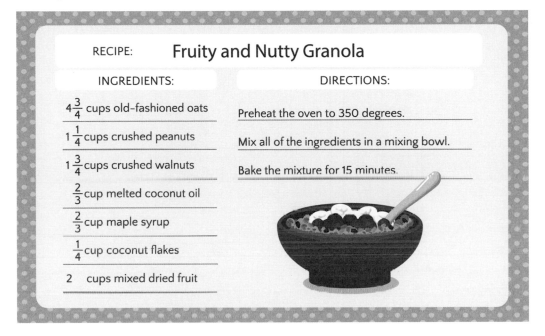

RECIPE: **Fruity and Nutty Granola**

INGREDIENTS:

$4\frac{3}{4}$ cups old-fashioned oats

$1\frac{1}{4}$ cups crushed peanuts

$1\frac{3}{4}$ cups crushed walnuts

$\frac{2}{3}$ cup melted coconut oil

$\frac{2}{3}$ cup maple syrup

$\frac{1}{4}$ cup coconut flakes

2   cups mixed dried fruit

DIRECTIONS:

Preheat the oven to 350 degrees.

Mix all of the ingredients in a mixing bowl.

Bake the mixture for 15 minutes.

Use the recipe to answer each question.

First, Willow and her mom pour the oats and the crushed peanuts into a bowl. How many cups of ingredients are in the bowl?

_____

Next, they add the crushed walnuts to the bowl. How many cups of ingredients are in the bowl now?

_____

Willow and her mom really like coconut flakes! So, they triple the amount of coconut flakes in the recipe. How many cups of coconut flakes do they use?

_____

Willow's mom has $2\frac{1}{3}$ cups of coconut oil. How much coconut oil will she have after she makes the granola?

_____

IXL.com
skill ID

7B3

> **Let's Learn!**
>
> Fractions are related to decimals. To get ready for decimals, practice writing fractions that use tenths and hundredths.
>
>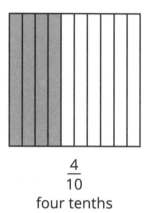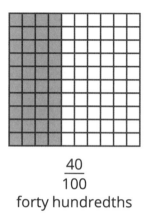
>
> $\dfrac{4}{10}$ $\dfrac{40}{100}$
>
> four tenths   forty hundredths

Write the fraction shown.

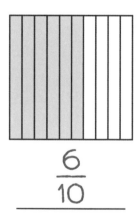

$\dfrac{6}{10}$

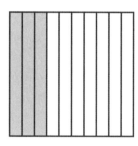

_____

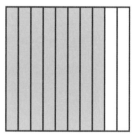

_____

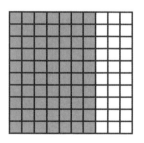

_____

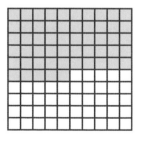

_____

_____

Let's Learn!

Decimals represent parts of wholes, just like fractions! You can use a place value chart to write the decimal. Try it for $\frac{46}{100}$. It is made up of 4 tenths and 6 hundredths.

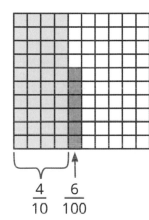

Ones		Tenths	Hundredths
0	.	4	6

Write each fraction as a decimal.

$\frac{3}{10}$ = __0.3__

$\frac{8}{10}$ = _____

$\frac{96}{100}$ = _____

$\frac{4}{10}$ = _____

$\frac{25}{100}$ = _____

$\frac{6}{10}$ = _____

$\frac{48}{100}$ = _____

$\frac{9}{100}$ = _____

IXL.com
skill ID
6P7

Write the missing fractions and decimals.

Fraction	Decimal
$\frac{59}{100}$	0.59
	0.23
$\frac{15}{100}$	
	0.9
$\frac{7}{100}$	
	0.81
$\frac{2}{10}$	
	0.03

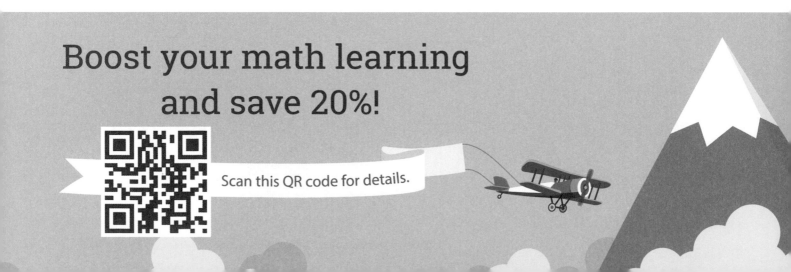

Let's Learn!

Some fractions have denominators that aren't 10 or 100, but you can still write them as decimals! First, find an equivalent fraction with a denominator of 10 or 100. Then you can write the decimal using place value.

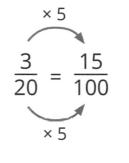

$$\frac{3}{20} = \frac{15}{100}$$

× 5 (above), × 5 (below)

Ones		Tenths	Hundredths
0	.	1	5

Write an equivalent fraction with a denominator of 10 or 100. Then write the fraction as a decimal.

$$\frac{3}{4} = \frac{75}{100} = 0.75$$

$$\frac{12}{25} = \underline{\hspace{2cm}} = \underline{\hspace{2cm}}$$

$$\frac{3}{5} = \underline{\hspace{2cm}} = \underline{\hspace{2cm}}$$

$$\frac{35}{50} = \underline{\hspace{2cm}} = \underline{\hspace{2cm}}$$

$$\frac{1}{4} = \underline{\hspace{2cm}} = \underline{\hspace{2cm}}$$

$$\frac{1}{2} = \underline{\hspace{2cm}} = \underline{\hspace{2cm}}$$

$$\frac{18}{20} = \underline{\hspace{2cm}} = \underline{\hspace{2cm}}$$

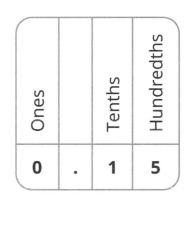

IXL.com
skill ID
6QG

Draw lines to match equivalent fractions and decimals.

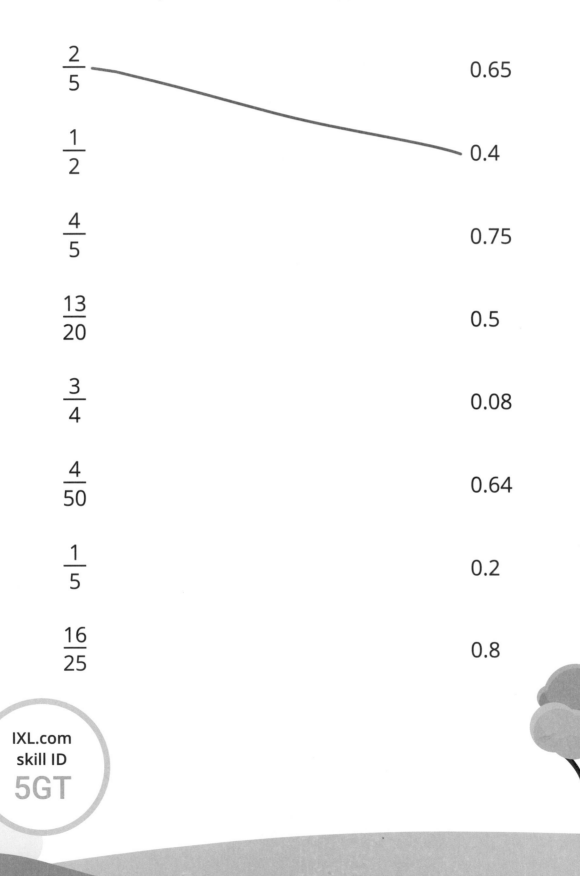

$\dfrac{2}{5}$ 0.65

$\dfrac{1}{2}$ 0.4

$\dfrac{4}{5}$ 0.75

$\dfrac{13}{20}$ 0.5

$\dfrac{3}{4}$ 0.08

$\dfrac{4}{50}$ 0.64

$\dfrac{1}{5}$ 0.2

$\dfrac{16}{25}$ 0.8

In each group, only two of the statements are correct. Cross out the incorrect statement.

$$\frac{2}{5} = 0.04$$ ~~crossed out~~

$$\frac{16}{20} = 0.80$$

$$\frac{4}{10} = 0.4$$

$$0.30 = \frac{15}{50}$$

$$0.18 = \frac{9}{50}$$

$$\frac{1}{4} = 0.20$$

$$\frac{3}{5} = 0.6$$

$$0.04 = \frac{10}{25}$$

$$\frac{11}{25} = 0.44$$

$$0.64 = \frac{32}{50}$$

$$\frac{14}{20} = 0.07$$

$$0.80 = \frac{20}{25}$$

$$\frac{1}{5} = 0.02$$

$$\frac{2}{25} = 0.08$$

$$0.38 = \frac{19}{50}$$

$$\frac{2}{4} = 0.50$$

$$0.70 = \frac{3}{25}$$

$$\frac{24}{25} = 0.96$$

Compare each pair of decimals. Fill in each circle with >, <, or =.

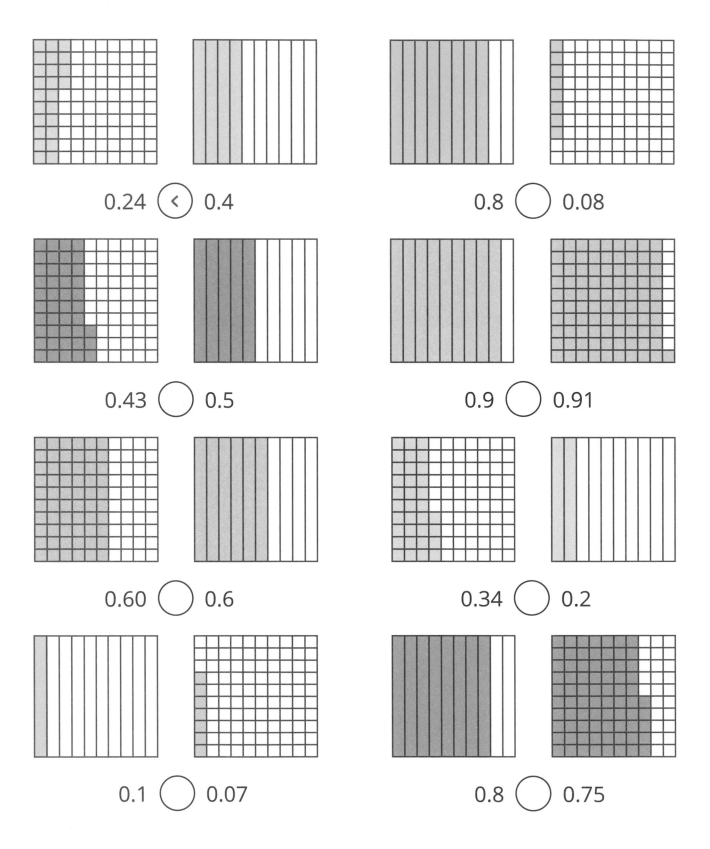

0.24 (<) 0.4

0.8 ( ) 0.08

0.43 ( ) 0.5

0.9 ( ) 0.91

0.60 ( ) 0.6

0.34 ( ) 0.2

0.1 ( ) 0.07

0.8 ( ) 0.75

Let's Learn!

You can compare decimals by comparing the digits in each place. Try it with 0.83 and 0.88.

0.83
0.88

Compare the **ones place** first. Since the digits are the same, keep going.

0.**8**3
0.**8**8

Compare the tenths place next. Since the digits are the same, keep going.

0.8**3**
0.8**8**

Compare the hundredths place next. The 3 is smaller than the 8. So, 0.83 < 0.88!

If the decimals have different numbers of digits, you can add zeros to the end of the shorter one. Then keep comparing! To see an example, look at the first problem below.

Compare each pair of decimals. Fill in each circle with >, <, or =.

0.32 (>) 0.30   0.75 ◯ 0.72   0.59 ◯ 0.8

0.39 ◯ 0.48   0.12 ◯ 0.1   0.30 ◯ 0.3

0.1 ◯ 0.09   0.65 ◯ 0.7   0.6 ◯ 0.06

2.1 ◯ 2.17   4.8 ◯ 4.80

Circle the greatest decimal in each row.

0.81	1.03	0.88
0.4	0.48	0.5
0.73	0.6	1.68
2.3	2.2	1.42
0.9	0.94	1.1

Circle the number that matches all of the clues.

I have a 2 in my tenths place.

I am less than 0.51.

I have a 5 in my hundredths place.

3.25	0.25	3.52
0.52	0.2	0.5
3.2	2.5	2.05

I am greater than 4.

I have a 9 in my hundredths place.

I am less than 4.5.

4.79	0.79	4.09
4.7	0.97	9.4
0.07	0.47	0.7

I am greater than 0.5, but less than 0.9.

I have an 8 in my tenths place.

I am equal to $\frac{4}{5}$.

0.85	8.5	0.5
5.8	0.58	0.08
0.8	8.05	0.05

Let's Learn!

You can use benchmark items to help you estimate customary units of length, weight, and volume.

Length	
Customary unit	**Benchmark**
Inch	Width of a quarter
Foot	Length of a loaf of bread
Yard	Length of a guitar
Mile	Length of about 15 football fields

Weight	
Customary unit	**Benchmark**
Ounce	Weight of an eraser
Pound	Weight of a can of soup
Ton	Weight of a small car

Volume	
Customary unit	**Benchmark**
Cup	Volume of a 1-cup measuring cup
Pint	Volume of a drinking glass
Quart	Volume of a large water bottle
Gallon	Volume of a milk jug

Circle the unit you would use to measure each length, weight, or volume.

The length of a dining room table: inches   (feet)

The weight of an adult dog: ounces   pounds

The volume of a bathtub: quarts   gallons

Circle the unit you would use to measure each length, weight, or volume.

The length of a picture frame: inches   yards

The weight of an elephant: ounces   tons

The volume of a cereal bowl: cups   quarts

The distance from New York to San Francisco: yards   miles

The weight of a pencil: ounces   pounds

The volume of a coffee mug: cups   quarts

The length of a soccer field: yards   miles

The weight of a sock: ounces   pounds

The volume of a trash can: pints   gallons

For more practice, visit IXL.com or the IXL mobile app and enter this code in the search bar.

IXL.com
skill ID
YYA

Let's Learn!

You can **convert**, or change, a measurement to a different unit. Let's try it with feet and inches.

There are 12 inches in a foot. So, 1 foot is the same as 12 inches. You can write feet as inches by multiplying the number of feet by 12. Look at the table to see how.

Feet	Inches
1	12
2	24
3	36

$1 \times 12 = 12$

$2 \times 12 = 24$

$3 \times 12 = 36$

Complete each table. Multiply to convert the first unit to the second unit.

There are 8 pints in a gallon.

Gallons	Pints
1	
2	
3	

There are 3 feet in a yard.

Yards	Feet
1	
2	
3	

There are 16 ounces in a pound.

Pounds	Ounces
1	
2	
3	

There are 2,000 pounds in a ton.

Tons	Pounds
1	
2	
3	

Let's Learn!

This table shows the relationships between several customary units. You can use this table to convert between units.

Customary conversion table	
1 foot (ft.) = 12 inches (in.)	1 ton = 2,000 lb.
1 yard (yd.) = 3 ft.	1 pint (pt.) = 2 cups (c.)
1 mile (mi.) = 5,280 ft.	1 quart (qt.) = 2 pt.
1 pound (lb.) = 16 ounces (oz.)	1 gallon (gal.) = 4 qt.

Multiply to convert each measurement.

154 yd. = ___462___ ft.

$154 \times 3 = 462$

5 gal. = _____ qt.

57 pt. = _____ c.

429 qt. = _____ pt.

4,500 yd. = _____ ft.

17 lb. = _____ oz.

36 lb. = _____ oz.

4 tons = _____ lb.

Answer each question.

Ms. Randolph bought 5 quarts of ice cream for her daughter's birthday party. How many pints of ice cream does she have?

_____

The art teacher at Windy Creek Elementary has eight 1-gallon bottles of glue in her closet. How many quarts of glue are in the closet?

_____

Penny, the African elephant that lives at Spring Creek Zoo, weighs 5 tons. How many pounds does Penny weigh?

_____

Amy adopted a pet pig and named him Wilson. Wilson weighs 14 pounds. How many ounces does Wilson weigh?

_____

Ryan's house is 4 miles away from his best friend Nathan's house. What is that distance in feet?

_____

INCHES TO FEET

You know how to convert feet to inches, but what about the other way around? If something is 24 inches long, how many feet is that? You can divide to find out!

Inches	Feet
12	1
24	2
36	3

12 inches ÷ 12 = 1 foot

24 inches ÷ 12 = 2 feet

36 inches ÷ 12 = 3 feet

In general, when you want to convert from a smaller unit to a larger unit, you can divide.

TRY IT YOURSELF!

Divide to convert each measurement.

58 pints = _____ quarts

36 feet = _____ yards

60 quarts = _____ gallons

72 inches = _____ feet

Let's Learn!

You can measure time using the units in the table. The table shows relationships between different units of time.

Time conversion table	
1 minute = 60 seconds	1 week = 7 days
1 hour = 60 minutes	1 year = 12 months
1 day = 24 hours	1 year = 52 weeks

Multiply to convert each measurement.

45 hours = __2,700__ minutes

$45 \times 60 = 2,700$

9 weeks = _____ days

7 minutes = _____ seconds

12 years = _____ months

3 years = _____ weeks

59 weeks = _____ days

27 days = _____ hours

24 hours = _____ minutes

Let's Learn!

You can use benchmark items to help you understand metric units of length, mass, and volume.

Length	
Metric unit	**Benchmark**
Millimeter	Thickness of a dime
Centimeter	Width of your index finger
Meter	Width of a doorway
Kilometer	Length that you can walk in about 10 minutes

Mass	
Metric unit	**Benchmark**
Gram	Mass of a paper clip
Kilogram	Mass of a wooden baseball bat

Volume	
Metric unit	**Benchmark**
Milliliter	Volume of 20 drops of water
Liter	Volume of a large water bottle

Circle the unit you would use to measure each length, mass, or volume.

The length of an ant: (millimeters) centimeters

The mass of your full backpack: grams kilograms

The volume of one dose of cough medicine: milliliters liters

Circle the unit you would use to measure each length, mass, or volume.

The width of a chapter book: centimeters   meters

The mass of a teabag: grams   kilograms

The volume of a punch bowl: milliliters   liters

The distance of a 20-minute bike ride: meters   kilometers

The mass of a bowling ball: grams   kilograms

The volume of a kitchen sink: milliliters   liters

The thickness of a quarter: millimeters   centimeters

The mass of a ping-pong ball: grams   kilograms

The volume of a perfume bottle: milliliters   liters

Complete each table. Multiply to convert the first unit to the second unit.

There are 1,000 milliliters in a liter.

Liters	Milliliters
1	
2	
3	
4	
5	

There are 10 millimeters in a centimeter.

Centimeters	Millimeters
1	
2	
3	
4	
5	

There are 100 centimeters in a meter.

Meters	Centimeters
1	
2	
3	
4	
5	

There are 1,000 grams in a kilogram.

Kilograms	Grams
1	
2	
3	
4	
5	

IXL.com
skill ID
YTJ

Let's Learn!

This table shows the relationships between several metric units. You can use this table to convert between units.

Metric conversion table	
1 centimeter (cm) = 10 millimeters (mm)	
1 meter (m) = 100 cm	1 kilogram (kg) = 1,000 grams (g)
1 kilometer (km) = 1,000 m	1 liter (L) = 1,000 milliliters (mL)

Multiply to convert each measurement.

49 L = _____49,000_____ mL

49 × 1,000 = 49,000

18 cm = _____ mm

36 kg = _____ g

5 km = _____ m

72 m = _____ cm

45 L = _____ mL

200 cm = _____ mm

582 kg = _____ g

620 L = _____ mL

IXL.com
skill ID
UL5

Answer each question.

Sally's pencil is 14 centimeters long. How many millimeters long is Sally's pencil?

_____

The top bunk of Malcolm's bunk beds holds 180 kilograms. How many grams can the top bunk hold?

_____

Kyle and his friends measured how far they could jump with a running head start. Kyle jumped 3 meters. How many centimeters did Kyle jump?

_____

Kelsey and her family drove 23 kilometers to go skiing. How many meters did they drive?

_____

During practice, Jordan's football team drank 25 liters of water. How many milliliters of water did the football team drink?

_____

Add to find the perimeter of each shape. If your answer is a fraction that is greater than 1, write it as a mixed number.

150 in.

64 in.   64 in.

150 in.

Perimeter = _____428 IN._____

125 yd.

125 yd.   125 yd.

125 yd.

Perimeter = _____

245 cm   245 cm

173 cm

Perimeter = _____

$\frac{7}{8}$ in.

$\frac{2}{8}$ in. $\frac{2}{8}$ in.

$\frac{7}{8}$ in.

Perimeter = _____

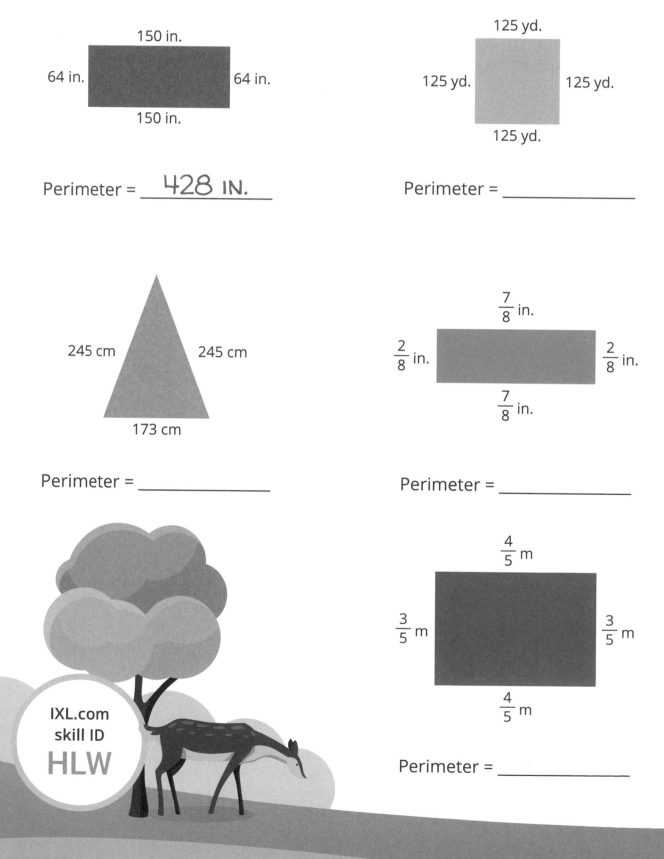

IXL.com
skill ID
HLW

$\frac{4}{5}$ m

$\frac{3}{5}$ m $\frac{3}{5}$ m

$\frac{4}{5}$ m

Perimeter = _____

Write the missing side lengths.

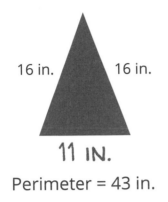

11 IN.

Perimeter = 43 in.

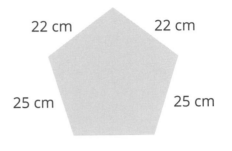

22 cm   22 cm

25 cm   25 cm

Perimeter = 113 cm

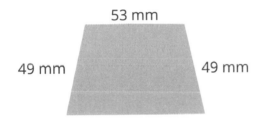

53 mm

49 mm   49 mm

Perimeter = 209 mm

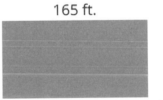

165 ft.

Perimeter = 488 ft.

Challenge yourself! Write the missing side lengths.

The length of a rectangle is 26 feet. Its perimeter is 88 feet. What is the width of the rectangle?

_____

The width of a rectangle is 298 centimeters. Its perimeter is 1,354 centimeters. What is the length of the rectangle?

_____

IXL.com
skill ID

QAC

Multiply to find the area of each rectangle. If your answer is a fraction that is greater than 1, write it as a mixed number.

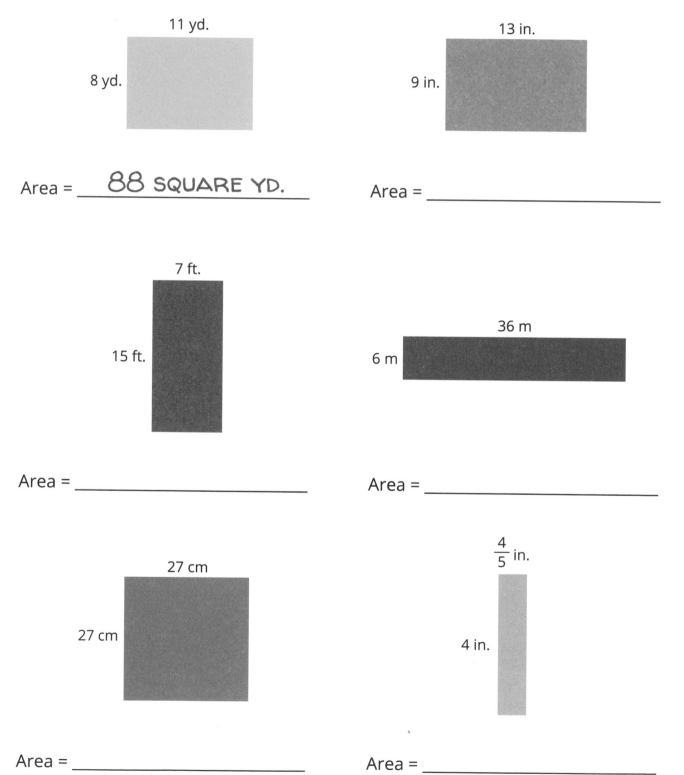

11 yd.

8 yd.

Area = _____88 SQUARE YD.____

13 in.

9 in.

Area = _____

7 ft.

15 ft.

Area = _____

36 m

6 m

Area = _____

27 cm

27 cm

Area = _____

$\frac{4}{5}$ in.

4 in.

Area = _____

Write the missing side lengths.

4 in.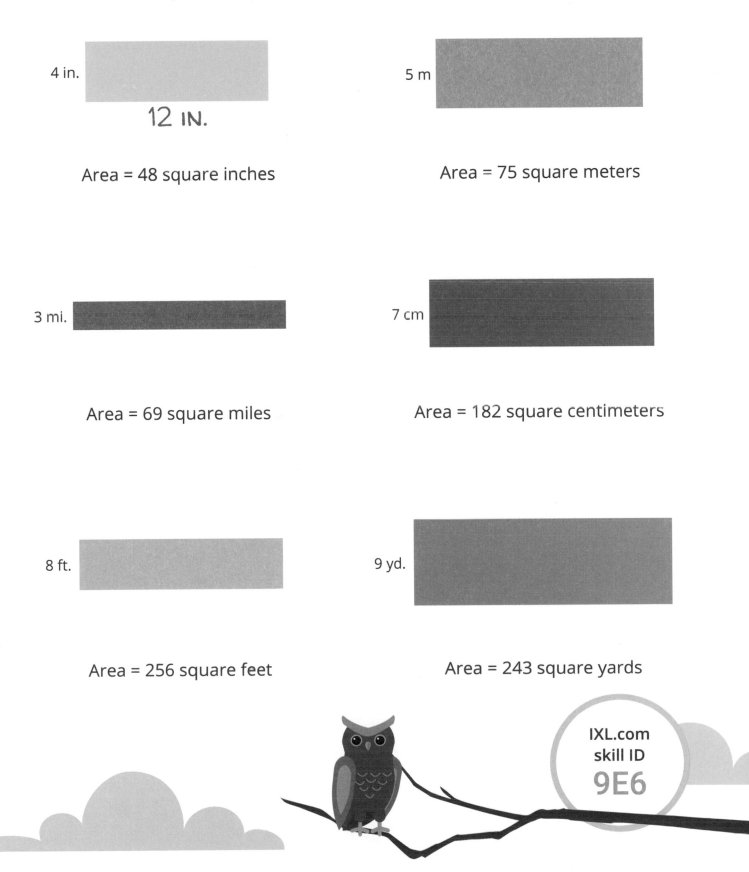

12 IN.

Area = 48 square inches

5 m

Area = 75 square meters

3 mi.

Area = 69 square miles

7 cm

Area = 182 square centimeters

8 ft.

Area = 256 square feet

9 yd.

Area = 243 square yards

Answer each question.

The balcony at Mr. Kerrington's beach house is 9 yards long and 5 yards wide. What is the area of the balcony?

_____

The city wants to put deer fencing around the community garden at Spring Meadow Park. The rectangular garden is 47 meters long and 33 meters wide. How many meters will be needed?

_____

Brandon and his dad are building a rectangular deck in their backyard. They want the deck to have a total area of 126 square feet. If the width of the deck is 6 feet, what is the length?

_____

A yield sign is a triangle with 36-inch sides. What is the perimeter of a yield sign?

_____

Ms. Bradley wants to cover all four of her basement walls with wallpaper. Each wall measures 24 feet by 8 feet. If Ms. Bradley bought 800 square feet of wallpaper, will she have enough to cover the area of all four walls?

_____

Find the area of each shape.

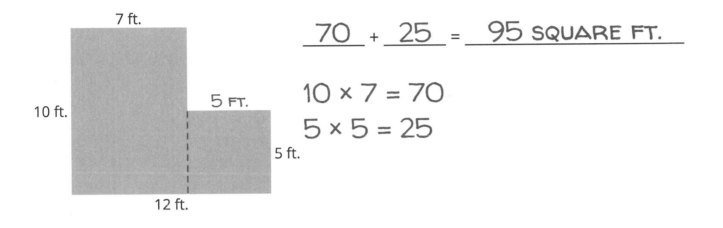

7 ft.

10 ft.

5 FT.

5 ft.

12 ft.

$\underline{\quad 70 \quad} + \underline{\quad 25 \quad} = \underline{\quad 95 \text{ SQUARE FT.} \quad}$

$10 \times 7 = 70$

$5 \times 5 = 25$

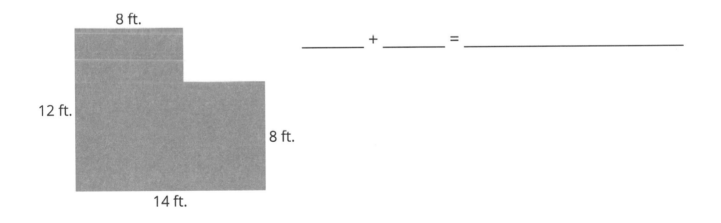

8 ft.

12 ft.

8 ft.

14 ft.

$\underline{\quad\quad} + \underline{\quad\quad} = \underline{\quad\quad\quad\quad}$

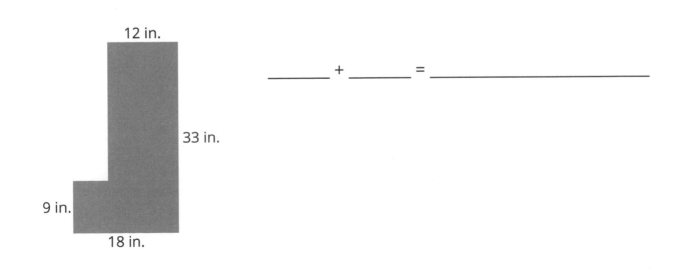

12 in.

33 in.

9 in.

18 in.

$\underline{\quad\quad} + \underline{\quad\quad} = \underline{\quad\quad\quad\quad}$

Find the area of each shape.

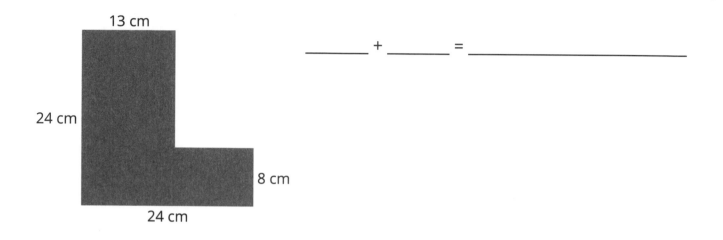

_____ + _____ = _____

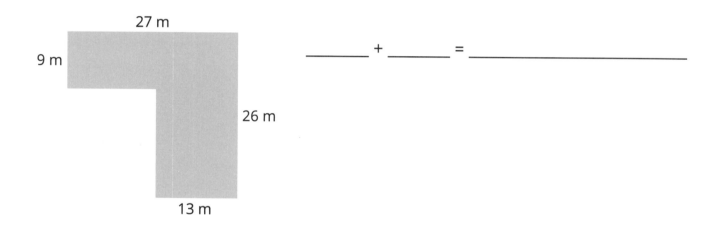

_____ + _____ = _____

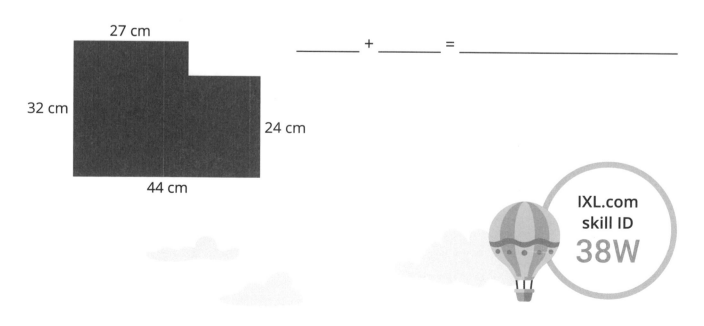

_____ + _____ = _____

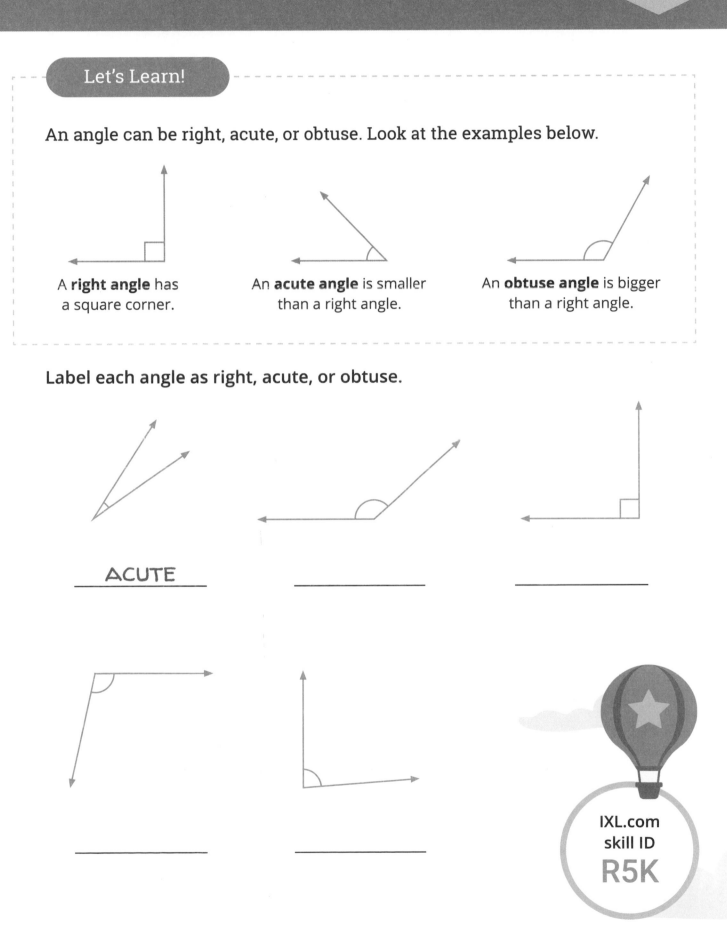

Let's Learn!

An angle can be right, acute, or obtuse. Look at the examples below.

A **right angle** has a square corner.

An **acute angle** is smaller than a right angle.

An **obtuse angle** is bigger than a right angle.

Label each angle as right, acute, or obtuse.

___ACUTE___

_____

_____

_____

_____

IXL.com
skill ID
R5K

Let's Learn!

Each triangle has a special name based on its angles.

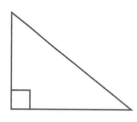

A **right triangle** has one right angle.

An **acute triangle** has three acute angles.

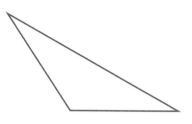

An **obtuse triangle** has one obtuse angle.

Label each triangle as right, acute, or obtuse.

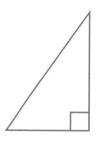

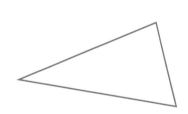

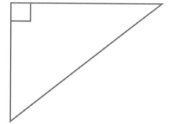

_____   _____   _____

_____   _____

IXL.com
skill ID
7QK

Let's Learn!

You can name triangles by their side lengths, too.

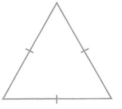

An **equilateral triangle**
has three equal sides.

An **isosceles triangle**
has two equal sides.

A **scalene triangle**
has no equal sides.

The markings in the pictures show which sides have equal lengths. Equal sides have the same markings.

Label each triangle as equilateral, isosceles, or scalene.

_____   _____   _____

_____   _____

IXL.com
skill ID
5UV

Draw lines to match each triangle to its name.

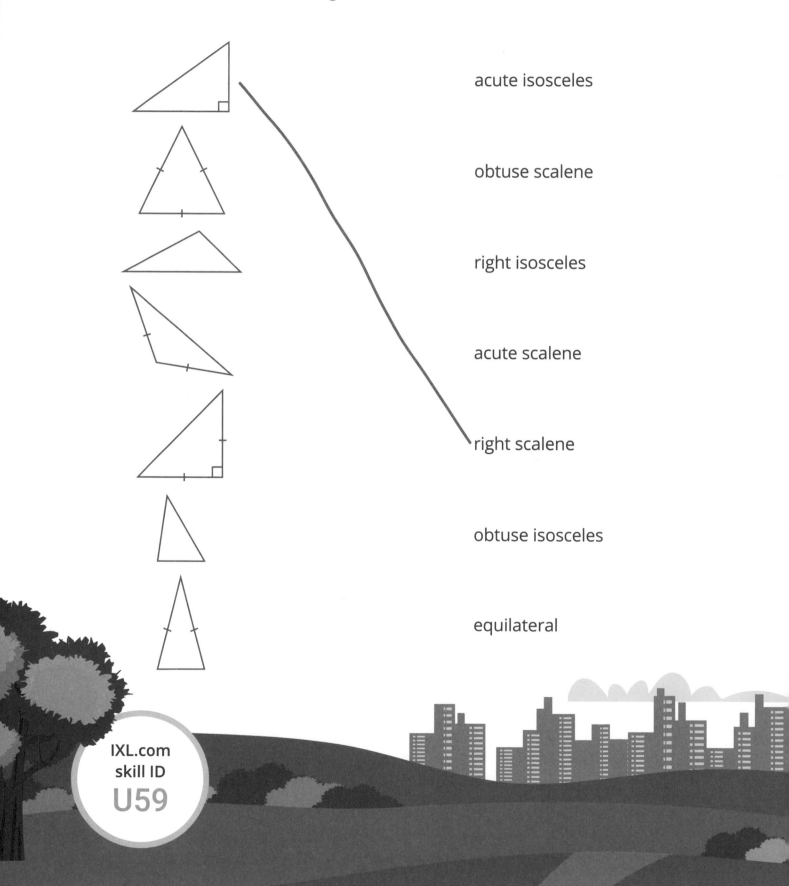

acute isosceles

obtuse scalene

right isosceles

acute scalene

right scalene

obtuse isosceles

equilateral

Let's Learn!

You can name pairs of lines by their relationship to each other.

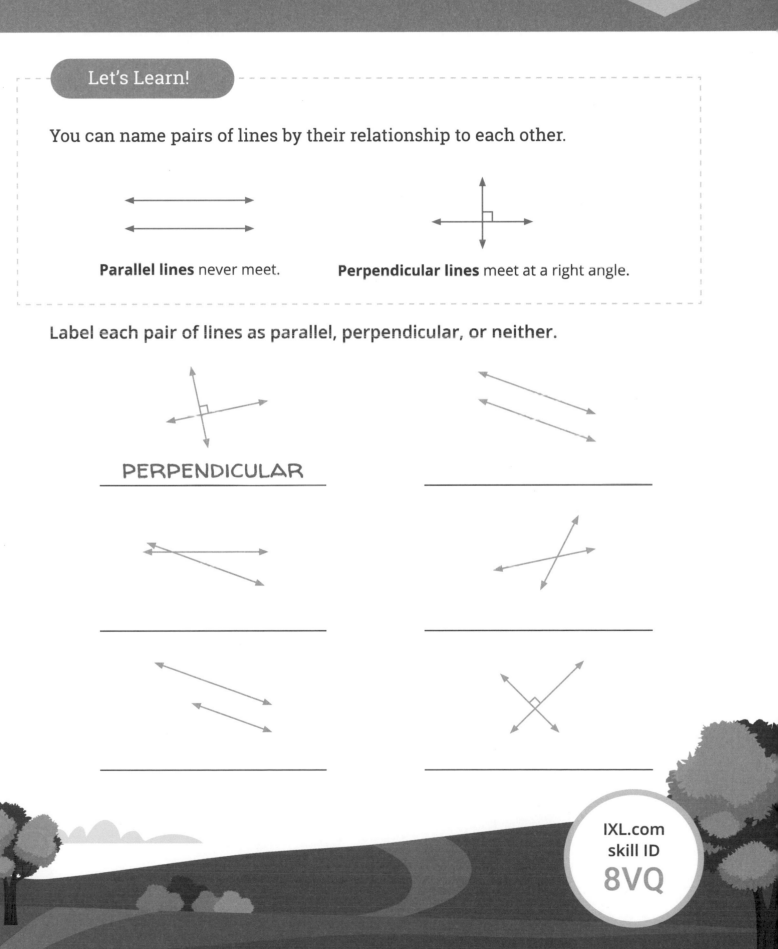

Parallel lines never meet.

Perpendicular lines meet at a right angle.

Label each pair of lines as parallel, perpendicular, or neither.

PERPENDICULAR

_____

_____

_____

_____

_____

_____

Tracey looks at a map of her hometown. Use the map to solve the problems.

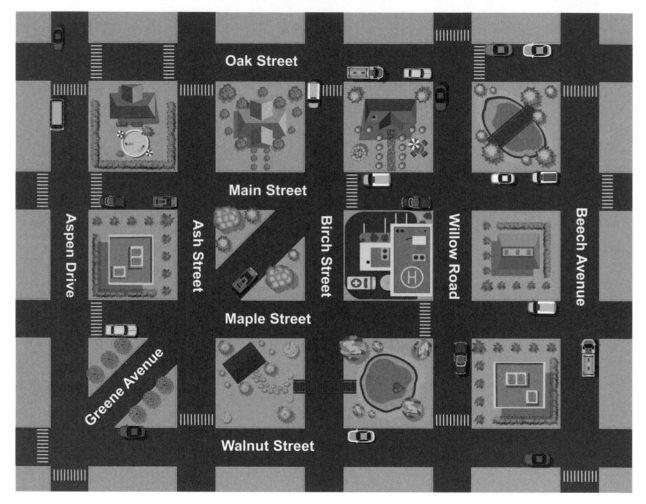

Name two streets that are perpendicular to each other.

_____

Name two streets that are parallel to Willow Road.

_____

Name two streets that are **not** parallel or perpendicular to each other.

_____

Name two streets that are perpendicular to Ash Street.

_____

Let's Learn!

Shapes can have special names and characteristics. A **parallelogram** is a shape with four sides and exactly two pairs of parallel sides.

This shape is a parallelogram because it has two pairs of parallel sides.

This shape is also a parallelogram because it has two pairs of parallel sides.

This shape is **not** a parallelogram, because it has only one pair of parallel sides.

Circle the parallelograms.

IXL.com skill ID DJ9

Let's Learn!

A parallelogram is a special type of **quadrilateral**, which is a shape that has four sides. Here are other special types of quadrilaterals.

A **parallelogram** has two pairs of parallel sides.

A **trapezoid** has one pair of parallel sides.

A **rectangle** is a parallelogram with four right angles.

A **rhombus** is a parallelogram with four equal side lengths.

A **square** is a parallelogram with four equal side lengths and four right angles. So, a square is also a rectangle and a rhombus.

Circle all of the rectangles.

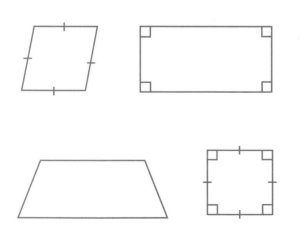

Circle all of the trapezoids.

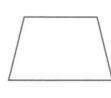

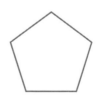

Circle all of the squares.

Circle all of the parallelograms.

Circle all of the quadrilaterals.

Circle all of the rhombuses.

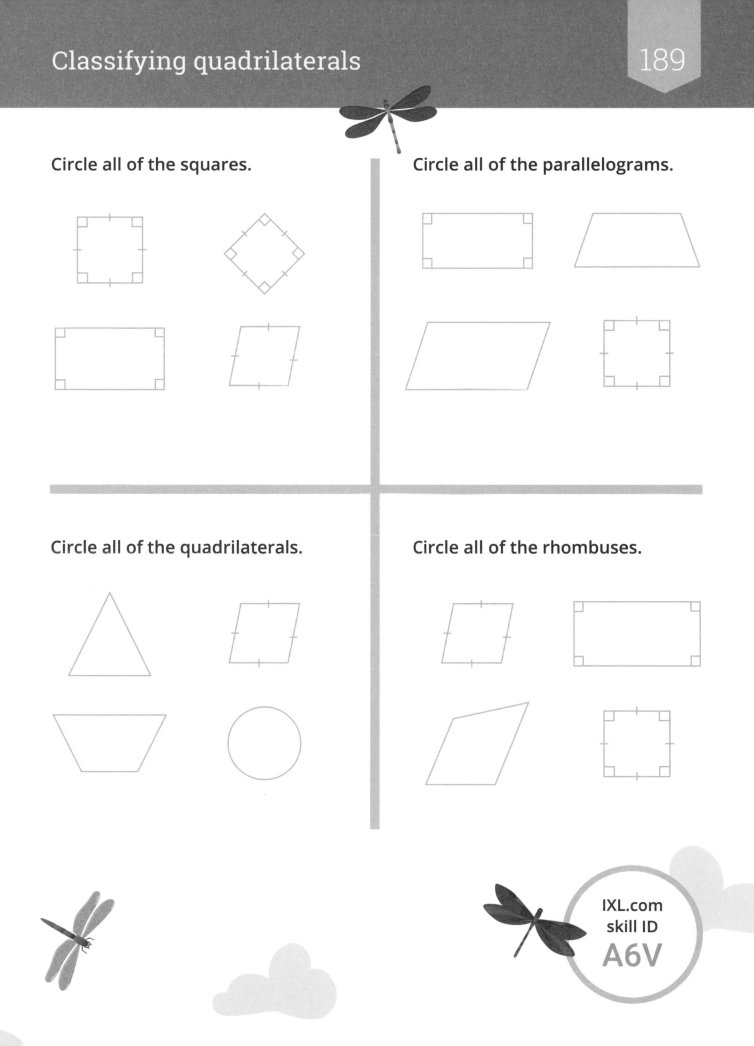

Let's Learn!

Angles are measured in degrees. A **protractor** is a tool that measures the number of degrees in an angle. Try it for the angle below.

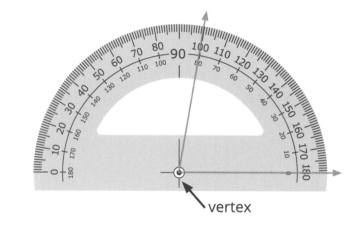

vertex

Put the **vertex** in the middle of the circle. Line up one side of the angle with 0 degrees. Then read the number at the other side of the angle.

Remember to use the same number scale in both places. If you start at the 0 in the inner circle, read the inner number at the other side of the angle.

So, this angle is 80 degrees, or 80°.

Write the measure of each angle.

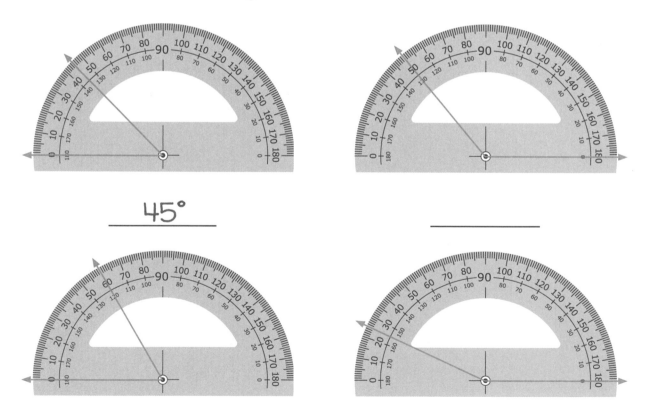

45°

_____

_____   _____

Write the measure of each angle.

Exploration Zone

DEGREES IN A CIRCLE

The circle below shows the degree measurements of different locations on a circle. If you start at 0° and go counterclockwise around the circle one time, you have gone 360°. So, one time around a circle is 360°.

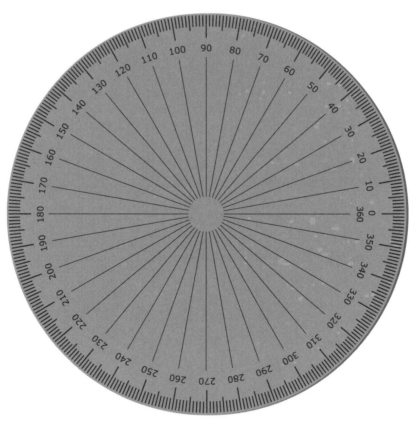

Use the circle to answer the questions below.

Start at 0°. If you go halfway around the circle, how many degrees is that?

_____180°_____

Start at 0°. If you go one-fourth of the way around the circle, how many degrees is that?

_____

Write acute, obtuse, or right to answer each question.

If you start at 0° and go one fourth of the way around the circle, what kind of angle do you make? Draw the angle.

_____

If you start at 0° and go one sixth of the way around the circle, what kind of angle do you make? Draw the angle.

_____

If you start at 0° and go one third of the way around the circle, what kind of angle do you make? Draw the angle.

_____

IXL.com
skill ID
RK8

Write the measure of each combined angle.

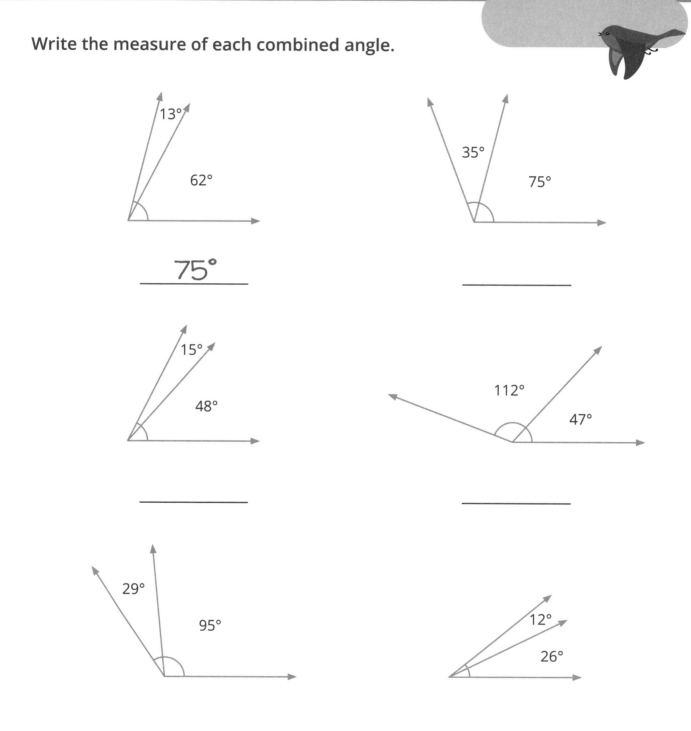

13°
62°
__75°__

35°
75°
_____

15°
48°
_____

112°
47°
_____

29°
95°
_____

12°
26°
_____

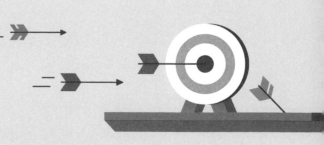

Write the measure of each missing angle.

Combined angle measure = 51°

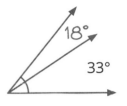

18°

33°

Combined angle measure = 134°

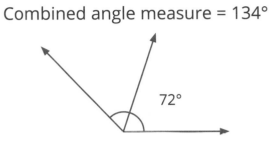

72°

Combined angle measure = 88°

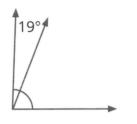

19°

Combined angle measure = 167°

47°

Combined angle measure = 140°

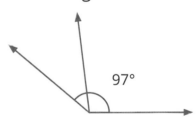

97°

Combined angle measure = 101°

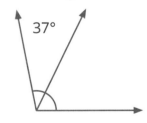

37°

Combined angle measure = 115°

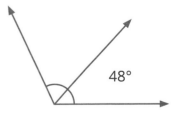

48°

A figure has **line symmetry** if it can be folded into matching parts. The fold line is called a line of symmetry.

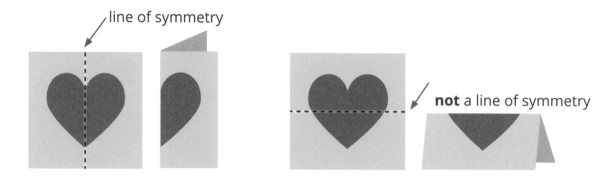

line of symmetry

not a line of symmetry

Circle each figure that shows a line of symmetry.

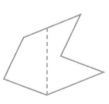
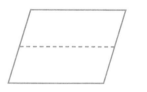
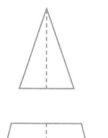

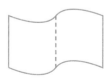

Draw a line of symmetry for each figure.

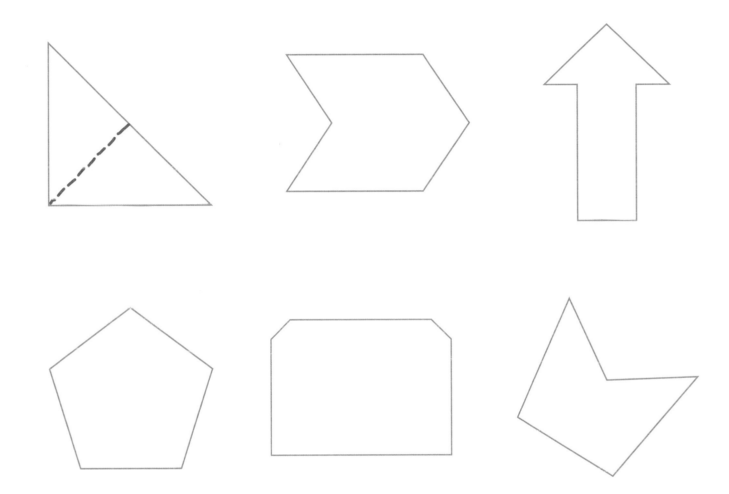

Let's Learn!

Some figures have more than one line of symmetry. For example, squares have four lines of symmetry.

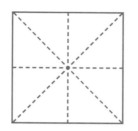

Draw as many lines of symmetry as possible for each figure.

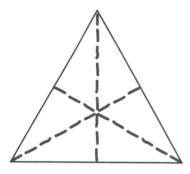

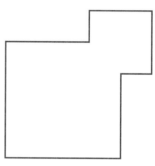

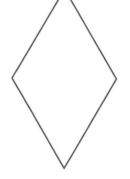

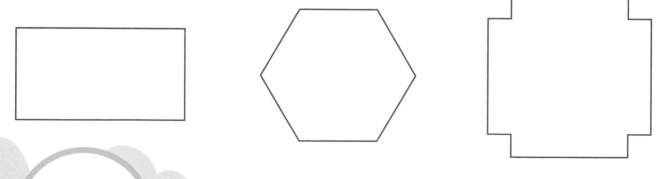

Complete each figure using the dotted line as a line of symmetry.

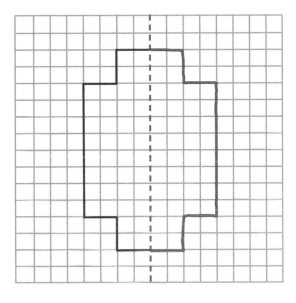

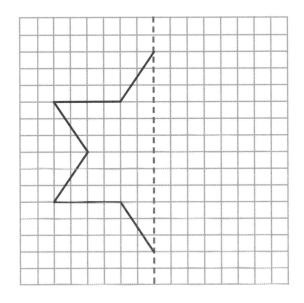

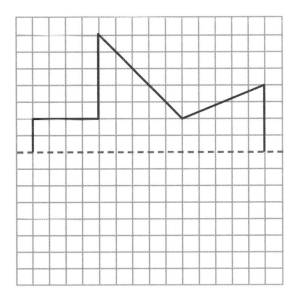

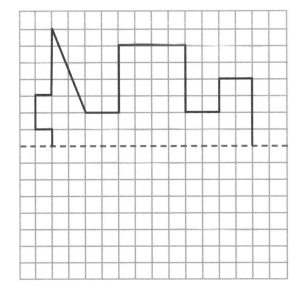

Complete each figure using the dotted lines as lines of symmetry.

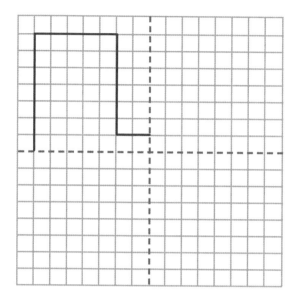

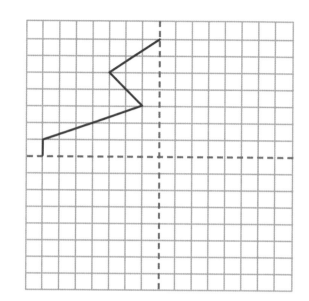

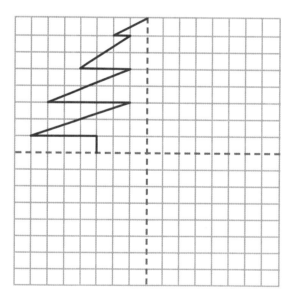

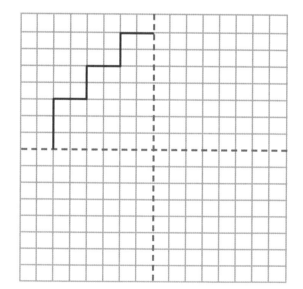

Time to review! Erica, Kaitlyn, Amelia, Charlotte, and Molly competed in the balance beam event at a gymnastics meet. Use the clues to solve the logic puzzle.

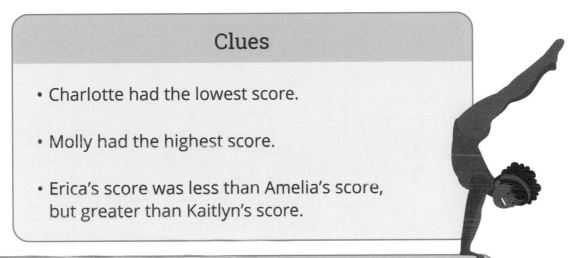

Clues

- Charlotte had the lowest score.

- Molly had the highest score.

- Erica's score was less than Amelia's score, but greater than Kaitlyn's score.

Score	Erica	Kaitlyn	Amelia	Charlotte	Molly
8.5					
7.95					
9.25					
8.7					
9.8					

Use your answers from the logic puzzle to solve the problem.

Another gymnast had a score that is less than Kaitlyn's score but greater than Charlotte's score. Write a possible score for this gymnast.

IXL.com
skill ID
LVX

_____

The Pleasant Hill Parks Committee hosts a spring carnival every year to raise money for the city's parks. The poster below shows the cost of admission passes and tickets.

Use the poster to answer each question.

The committee sold 429 pre-sale adult entry passes and 567 pre-sale child entry passes. How much money did the committee raise from pre-sale passes?

_____

Use the poster to answer each question.

On the day of the carnival, the committee made $1,218 on child entry passes. How many child passes did the committee sell on the day of the carnival?

_____

On the day of the carnival, the committee made $1,865 on adult entry passes. How many adult passes did the committee sell on the day of the carnival?

_____

Maria attended the carnival with her mom and 3 brothers. Her mom bought pre-sale admission passes for each person. She also bought 2 packs of 20 ride tickets. How much money did Maria's mom spend?

_____

Last year, Mrs. Carter bought 1 adult pass and 1 child pass on the day of the spring carnival. She also bought 2 packs of 20 ride tickets and a pack of 10 ride tickets. This year, she bought presale admission passes and a wristband. If the prices were the same last year as this year, how much money did Mrs. Carter save compared to last year?

_____

The Pleasant Hill Parks Committee raised a total of $19,637 from admission sales, ride ticket sales, and wristband sales. The committee made $5,504 on admissions sales and $5,193 on ride ticket sales. How much money did the committee make on wristband sales?

_____

IXL.com
skill ID
EA9

Julie is making her famous carrot cake cookies for family game night. Look at the ingredients she needs.

Carrot Cake Cookies
makes 24 cookies

COOKIES

$1\frac{1}{4}$ cups butter, softened	$2\frac{1}{4}$ cups all-purpose flour
$\frac{3}{4}$ cup sugar	1 teaspoon baking soda
$\frac{3}{4}$ cup packed brown sugar	$2\frac{1}{2}$ teaspoons cinnamon
2 eggs	$\frac{1}{2}$ teaspoon salt
$2\frac{1}{4}$ teaspoons vanilla extract	$1\frac{3}{4}$ cups carrots, grated

FROSTING

$3\frac{3}{4}$ cups powdered sugar	1 package cream cheese
$\frac{1}{4}$ cup butter, softened	$1\frac{1}{4}$ teaspoons vanilla extract

Use the recipe to answer each question.

Julie needs vanilla extract for both the cookies and the frosting. How much vanilla extract will she need in all? _____

Julie has only $\frac{3}{4}$ of a cup of flour in her cupboard. She is going to borrow flour from her neighbor. How much flour will she need to borrow?

_____

IXL.com
skill ID
LYR

Keep going! Use the recipe to answer each question. If your answer is a fraction greater than 1, write it as a mixed number.

Julie makes the cookies first. She mixes the sugar, brown sugar, and flour in a bowl. How many cups of ingredients are in the bowl?

_____

Julie can find only a $\frac{1}{4}$ -teaspoon measuring spoon. She fills the spoon with salt 2 times. Does she measure the correct amount of salt?

_____

Julie decides to make the carrot cake cookie recipe for her school's bake sale. She will make a triple batch of the cookies. **Help Julie finish writing the amounts of each ingredient she will need to make three times as many cookies as the original recipe. If your answer is greater than 1, write it as a mixed number or whole number.**

Carrot Cake Cookies
makes 72 cookies

COOKIES

$3\frac{3}{4}$ cups butter, softened

_____ cups sugar

_____ cups packed brown sugar

_____ eggs

$6\frac{3}{4}$ teaspoons vanilla extract

$6\frac{3}{4}$ cups all-purpose flour

_____ teaspoons baking soda

$7\frac{1}{2}$ teaspoons cinnamon

_____ teaspoons salt

$5\frac{1}{4}$ cups carrots, grated

FROSTING

$11\frac{1}{4}$ cups powdered sugar

_____ cup butter, softened

_____ packages cream cheese

$3\frac{3}{4}$ teaspoons vanilla extract

Mr. Walker is buying flooring for his new house. The picture below shows the layout of his house.

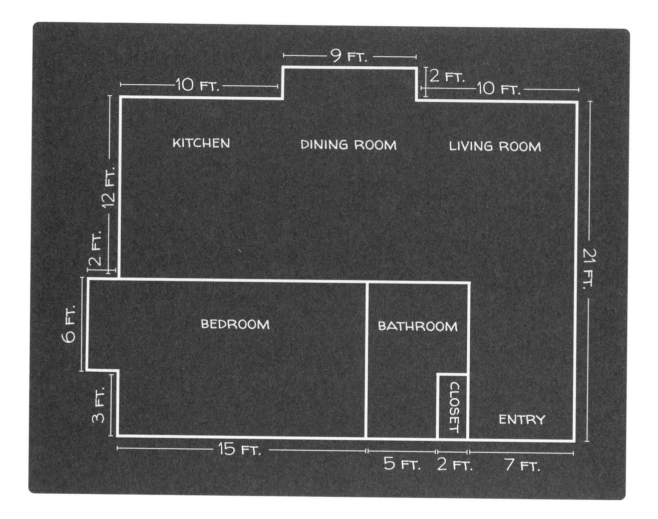

Use the picture to answer each question.

Mr. Walker wants to put carpet in the bedroom. How many square feet of carpet will he need?

_____

The cost of carpet is $2 per square foot. How much money will he spend on carpet?

_____

Use the picture to answer each question.

Mr. Walker wants to put tile in the bathroom and closet. How many square feet of tile will he need?

_____

The home improvement store sells boxes of tile. Each box contains 9 tiles that are 1 square foot each. Each box of tile costs $16. How much money will he spend on tile?

_____

Mr. Walker wants to put hardwood floors in the rest of the house. How many square feet of hardwood will he need to buy?

_____

The cost of hardwood is $5 per square foot. How much money will he spend on hardwood?

_____

What is the total area of Mr. Walker's new house?

_____

Answer key

PAGE 2

hundreds
ten thousands
millions

tens
thousands
hundred thousands

PAGE 3

70	9,000	8
30,000	40,000	300
20	1,000	100,000
4,000,000	100,000	2,000,000
700	80	500,000

PAGE 4

5,292
200

35,141
30,000

704,005
4,000

PAGE 5

5,000 + 400 + 7
10,000 + 7,000 + 800 + 40 + 3
40,000 + 8,000 + 4
200,000 + 1,000 + 60 + 5

4,275
283,581
56,083
602,390

PAGE 6

176,900
61,701
425,000
900,000
300,600

twenty thousand five hundred eighty
six hundred forty-eight thousand
ninety-one thousand two hundred
seven hundred thousand thirty

PAGE 7

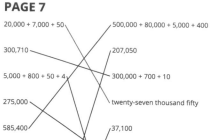
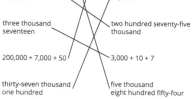

20,000 + 7,000 + 50
300,710
5,000 + 800 + 50 + 4
275,000
585,400
three thousand seventeen
200,000 + 7,000 + 50
thirty-seven thousand one hundred

500,000 + 80,000 + 5,000 + 400
207,050
300,000 + 700 + 10
twenty-seven thousand fifty
37,100
two hundred seventy-five thousand
3,000 + 10 + 7
five thousand eight hundred fifty-four

PAGE 8

1,200 = 12 hundreds	50 tens = 500
36 hundreds = 3,600	78 tens = 780
42 hundreds = 4,200	920 = 92 tens
890 = 89 tens	63 tens = 630
300 = 30 tens	72 hundreds = 7,200

PAGE 9

37 hundreds = 3,700	54 tens = 540
24 hundreds = 2,400	83 tens = 830
68 tens = 680	74 hundreds = 7,400
91 hundreds = 9,100	26 tens = 260
95 tens = 950	32 hundreds = 3,200
70 tens = 700	95 hundreds = 9,500

PAGE 10

14,573 < 18,009	10,300 > 7,890
16,421 > 16,391	45,912 > 44,879
52,581 = 52,581	60,120 > 59,938
79,402 < 79,412	97,241 < 100,325

PAGE 11

67,788 < 156,788	397,110 > 387,110
640,920 > 640,918	578,263 > 67,578
567,352 < 567,452	180,436 = 180,436
128,728 > 128,278	847,032 < 847,100
198,900 < 200,100	664,215 > 662,415

Answers may vary. Some possible answers are shown below.

| 19,236 < 19,237 | 47,195 > 47,194 |
| 298,403 > 298,402 | 634,195 < 634,196 |

PAGE 12

7,892	10,985	12,521
98,354	98,954	100,002
102,825	102,964	120,723
641,297	641,306	642,050
854,458	854,462	854,500
987,002	993,150	1,000,000

PAGE 13

October
Flat Peak
Chicago
Houston

PAGE 14

700	200
5,800	3,900
34,600	98,600
126,400	425,100
542,300	607,500

PAGE 15

7,000	10,000
18,000	28,000
384,000	405,000
619,000	933,000

40,000	90,000
70,000	210,000
590,000	840,000
1,180,000	

PAGE 16

43,243
286,605
654,181

PAGE 17

10,000 + 80,000 = 90,000
60,000 − 30,000 = 30,000
20,000 + 50,000 = 70,000
80,000 − 30,000 = 50,000

200,000 + 300,000 = 500,000
800,000 − 400,000 = 400,000
300,000 + 400,000 = 700,000
800,000 − 200,000 = 600,000

PAGE 18

53,774 + 42,417 96,191	76,385 + 32,914 109,299	43,480 + 38,239 81,719
24,386 + 71,873 96,259	13,416 + 85,959 99,375	59,827 + 37,168 96,995

PAGE 19

17,342 + 47,577 64,919	39,660 + 31,588 71,248	37,726 + 25,945 63,671
49,737 + 28,476 78,213	19,379 + 80,184 99,563	63,048 + 28,986 92,034
422,685 + 121,482 544,167	354,984 + 101,618 456,602	865,908 + 125,915 991,823
136,199 + 561,774 697,973	720,856 + 265,309 986,165	269,859 + 615,644 885,503

PAGE 20

595,289 + 213,716 809,005	46,204 + 82,527 128,731	434,712 + 264,524 699,236
53,532 + 74,894 128,426	26,528 + 52,613 79,141	436,467 + 171,889 608,356
257,823 + 731,341 989,164	472,724 + 466,426 939,150	24,485 + 84,214 108,699

PAGE 21

2,827 1,281 + 2,472 6,580	5,344 3,853 + 4,081 13,278
36,832 37,903 + 52,492 127,227	59,238 17,442 + 65,902 142,582
83,398 74,550 + 26,492 184,440	92,244 53,760 + 88,238 234,242

PAGE 21, continued

272,504 404,395 + 180,478 857,377	368,734 198,049 + 274,376 841,159

PAGE 22

36,375 − 12,642 23,733	52,905 − 14,642 38,263	77,511 − 32,415 45,096
63,242 − 56,728 6,514	97,432 − 28,871 68,561	86,672 − 24,913 61,759

PAGE 23

71,270 − 32,425 38,845	54,183 − 30,365 23,818	41,423 − 36,390 5,033
97,541 − 43,663 53,878	82,476 − 51,806 30,670	74,203 − 25,097 49,106
433,560 − 180,248 253,312	747,852 − 433,678 314,174	824,913 − 186,672 638,241
923,139 − 637,714 285,425	878,761 − 359,584 519,177	

PAGE 24

	START		
283,900 − 173,764 110,136	780,547 − 479,347 301,200	933,114 − 634,790 298,324	888,757 − 665,860 222,897
614,288 − 490,919 123,369	649,696 − 447,932 201,764	490,996 − 308,064 182,932	541,343 − 356,948 184,395
943,158 − 741,852 201,306	945,116 − 637,212 307,904	823,804 − 519,923 303,881	745,029 − 452,645 292,384
435,773 − 210,833 224,940	1,000,000 − 780,575 219,425	841,682 − 644,431 197,251	744,297 − 536,927 207,370

FINISH

PAGE 25

72,092 − 42,153 29,939	98,261 − 37,454 60,807	204,374 − 92,296 112,078	131,472 − 67,394 64,078
239,421 − 237,309 2,112	What is the smallest answer on this page? 2,112		657,072 − 649,471 7,601
127,382 − 97,456 29,926			841,053 − 639,844 201,209
451,928 − 427,392 24,536	163,008 − 71,753 91,255	640,859 − 619,779 21,080	785,148 − 767,093 18,055

PAGE 26

757,545 − 148,963 608,582	284,991 + 452,568 737,559	885,027 − 310,459 574,568
385,920 + 488,986 874,906	738,060 − 455,853 282,207	368,691 + 497,483 866,174
433,951 − 178,304 255,647	690,467 + 258,658 949,125	746,206 − 619,739 126,467

PAGE 27

1 5	2	7	3		2 4
4					5
3 5	4 7	3	4	6 4	4
	0				3
	3				1
	6				
5 6	5	7	2	6 1	2
	1				
7 4	8	2	7	7	3

PAGE 28

736,657 < 773,661

639,446 < 642,266

306,865 > 304,498

243,920 < 300,745

Answer key

PAGE 29

6,107 shortcakes

8,288 feet

274,500 lollipops

307,309 items

337,815 adults

PAGE 30

21,294 creatures

3,894 empty seats

169,850 pounds

$386,000

PAGE 31

3 rows of 4 = 12   2 rows of 3 = 6

3 x 4 = 12   2 × 3 = 6

2 rows of 4 = 8   3 rows of 3 = 9

2 × 4 = 8   3 × 3 = 9

4 rows of 5 = 20

4 × 5 = 20

PAGE 32

2 rows of 6 = 12   3 rows of 5 = 15

2 × 6 = 12   3 × 5 = 15

5 rows of 5 = 25   3 rows of 6 = 18

5 × 5 = 25   3 × 6 = 18

3 rows of 8 = 24   4 rows of 6 = 24

3 × 8 = 24   4 × 6 = 24

PAGE 33

3 × 7 = 21   5 × 4 = 20   4 × 7 = 28

10 × 11 = 110   6 × 12 = 72   1 × 9 = 9

12 × 0 = 0   10 × 2 = 20   9 × 6 = 54

5 × 10 = 50   8 × 4 = 32   6 × 11 = 66

3 × 2 = 6   7 × 8 = 56   9 × 7 = 63

PAGE 34

1 × 5 = 5   7 × 6 = 42   10 × 7 = 70

4 × 9 = 36   12 × 3 = 36   2 × 9 = 18

11 × 8 = 88   5 × 8 = 40   4 × 4 = 16

8 × 9 = 72   6 × 5 = 30   2 × 12 = 24

3 × 10 = 30   8 × 3 = 24   6 × 8 = 48

PAGE 35

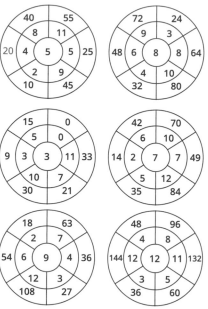

PAGE 36

2 × 8 = 16   6 × 7 = 42   6 × 10 = 60

1 × 4 = 4   7 × 12 = 84   12 × 5 = 60

7 × 0 = 0   2 × 12 = 24   10 × 10 = 100

11 × 2 = 22   4 × 11 = 44   8 × 8 = 64

7 × 4 = 28   8 × 6 = 48   5 × 9 = 45

3 × 12 = 36   8 × 7 = 56   5 × 6 = 30

PAGE 37

54 years old

40 volunteers

72 slices

27 paper cranes

96 people

PAGE 38

7 × 40 = 280

2 × 60 = 120

6 × 600 = 3,600

6 × 300 = 1,800

3 × 5,000 = 15,000

9 × 60 = 540

8 × 2,000 = 16,000

4 × 90,000 = 360,000

7 × 7,000 = 49,000

4 × 40,000 = 160,000

5 × 6,000 = 30,000

PAGE 39

4 × 17 is about 4 × 20 = 80

7 × 29 is about 7 × 30 = 210

9 × 53 is about 9 × 50 = 450

2 × 72 is about 2 × 70 = 140

6 × 37 is about 6 × 40 = 240

8 × 81 is about 8 × 80 = 640

5 × 41 is about 5 × 40 = 200

3 × 98 is about 3 × 100 = 300

PAGE 40

Steps may vary.

6 × 37 = 6 × (30 + 7)

6 × 37 = (6 × 30) + (6 × 7)

6 × 37 = 180 + 42

6 × 37 = 222

9 × 52 = 9 × (50 + 2)

9 × 52 = (9 × 50) + (9 × 2)

9 × 52 = 450 + 18

9 × 52 = 468

PAGE 41

Steps may vary.

5 × 87 = 5 × (80 + 7)

5 × 87 = (5 × 80) + (5 × 7)

5 × 87 = 400 + 35

5 × 87 = 435

7 × 29 = 7 × (20 + 9)

7 × 29 = (7 × 20) + (7 × 9)

7 × 29 = 140 + 63

7 × 29 = 203

4 × 95 = 4 × (90 + 5)

4 × 95 = (4 × 90) + (4 × 5)

4 × 95 = 360 + 20

4 × 95 = 380

PAGE 42

Steps may vary.

5 × 325 = 5 × (300 + 20 + 5)

5 × 325 = (5 × 300) + (5 × 20) + (5 × 5)

5 × 325 = 1,500 + 100 + 25

5 × 325 = 1,625

PAGE 42, *continued*

3 × 654 = 3 × (600 + 50 + 4)

3 × 654 = (3 × 600) + (3 × 50) + (3 × 4)

3 × 654 = 1,800 + 150 + 12

3 × 654 = 1,962

7 × 263 = 7 × (200 + 60 + 3)

7 × 263 = (7 × 200) + (7 × 60) + (7 × 3)

7 × 263 = 1,400 + 420 + 21

7 × 263 = 1,841

PAGE 43

4 × 57 = 228   7 × 48 = 336

8 × 39 = 312   6 × 72 = 432

4 × 154 = 616   3 × 293 = 879

9 × 244 = 2,196   7 × 518 = 3,626

PAGE 44

41	34	91
× 5	× 2	× 4
205	68	364

83	23	21
× 2	× 3	× 8
166	69	168

PAGE 45

94	61	51
× 2	× 5	× 7
188	305	357

82	54	72
× 4	× 2	× 3
328	108	216

61	71	62
× 9	× 8	× 4
549	568	248

53	64	81
× 3	× 2	× 6
159	128	486

PAGE 46

63	48	37
× 5	× 2	× 3
315	96	111

46	86	97
× 5	× 4	× 8
230	344	776

PAGE 47

43	82	19
× 4	× 7	× 5
172	574	95

35	38	26
× 8	× 3	× 6
280	114	156

29	53	45
× 9	× 7	× 4
261	371	180

65	84	
× 5	× 6	
325	504	

PAGE 48

563	433	702
× 3	× 2	× 4
1,689	866	2,808

942	203	824
× 4	× 8	× 5
3,768	1,624	4,120

532	173	608
× 6	× 9	× 7
3,192	1,557	4,256

837	754	385
× 6	× 8	× 9
5,022	6,032	3,465

PAGE 49

319	335	509
× 4	× 3	× 2
1,276	1,005	1,018

625	623	718
× 6	× 8	× 5
3,750	4,984	3,590

407	257	876
× 7	× 9	× 4
2,849	2,313	3,504

674	795	494
× 7	× 5	× 3
4,718	3,975	1,482

PAGE 50

3,841	5,132	3,812
× 2	× 4	× 5
7,682	20,528	19,060

5,192	1,872	1,453
× 3	× 8	× 7
15,576	14,976	10,171

2,654	4,639	3,762
× 6	× 9	× 4
15,924	41,751	15,048

6,725	5,913	6,670
× 5	× 8	× 3
33,625	47,304	20,010

3,943	7,527	
× 6	× 9	
23,658	67,743	

PAGE 51

William's race number is 2,196.

Olivia's race number is 3,540.

Emma's race number is 3,896.

Jayden's race number is 1,770.

Noah's race number is 1,286.

PAGE 52

84 bags of popcorn

175 bowls

368 animal fossils

1,312 seats

15,840 feet

PAGE 53

20 × 30 = 600

40 × 60 = 2,400

80 × 20 = 1,600

50 × 70 = 3,500

30 × 30 = 900

80 × 60 = 4,800

80 × 80 = 6,400

90 × 60 = 5,400

40 × 70 = 2,800

90 × 40 = 3,600

80 × 50 = 4,000

70 × 90 = 6,300

Answer key

PAGE 54

$$\begin{array}{r} 27 \\ \times\ 13 \\ \hline 351 \end{array}$$

$$\begin{array}{r} 81 \\ \times\ 74 \\ \hline 5{,}994 \end{array}$$

$$\begin{array}{r} 52 \\ \times\ 38 \\ \hline 1{,}976 \end{array}$$

PAGE 55

$$\begin{array}{r} 41 \\ \times\ 26 \\ \hline 1{,}066 \end{array}$$

$$\begin{array}{r} 14 \\ \times\ 34 \\ \hline 476 \end{array}$$

$$\begin{array}{r} 45 \\ \times\ 46 \\ \hline 2{,}070 \end{array}$$

$$\begin{array}{r} 92 \\ \times\ 54 \\ \hline 4{,}968 \end{array}$$

$$\begin{array}{r} 75 \\ \times\ 61 \\ \hline 4{,}575 \end{array}$$

$$\begin{array}{r} 62 \\ \times\ 16 \\ \hline 992 \end{array}$$

$$\begin{array}{r} 22 \\ \times\ 97 \\ \hline 2{,}134 \end{array}$$

$$\begin{array}{r} 76 \\ \times\ 32 \\ \hline 2{,}432 \end{array}$$

$$\begin{array}{r} 36 \\ \times\ 53 \\ \hline 1{,}908 \end{array}$$

PAGE 56

$$\begin{array}{r} 35 \\ \times\ 42 \\ \hline 1{,}470 \end{array}$$

$$\begin{array}{r} 29 \\ \times\ 85 \\ \hline 2{,}465 \end{array}$$

$$\begin{array}{r} 84 \\ \times\ 43 \\ \hline 3{,}612 \end{array}$$

$$\begin{array}{r} 73 \\ \times\ 37 \\ \hline 2{,}701 \end{array}$$

$$\begin{array}{r} 27 \\ \times\ 58 \\ \hline 1{,}566 \end{array}$$

$$\begin{array}{r} 39 \\ \times\ 57 \\ \hline 2{,}223 \end{array}$$

$$\begin{array}{r} 79 \\ \times\ 46 \\ \hline 3{,}634 \end{array}$$

$$\begin{array}{r} 49 \\ \times\ 65 \\ \hline 3{,}185 \end{array}$$

$$\begin{array}{r} 68 \\ \times\ 44 \\ \hline 2{,}992 \end{array}$$

$$\begin{array}{r} 67 \\ \times\ 93 \\ \hline 6{,}231 \end{array}$$

$$\begin{array}{r} 77 \\ \times\ 64 \\ \hline 4{,}928 \end{array}$$

$$\begin{array}{r} 83 \\ \times\ 92 \\ \hline 7{,}636 \end{array}$$

PAGE 57

432 hamburger buns

576 photos

300 pounds

$378

1,504 marshmallows

PAGE 58

Planters, since she made $264 selling vases and $272 selling planters.

1,235 chairs

$515

3,065 comic books

PAGE 59

2 × 3 = 6

6 ÷ 2 = 3

3 × 3 = 9

9 ÷ 3 = 3

3 × 6 = 18

18 ÷ 3 = 6

2 × 4 = 8

8 ÷ 2 = 4

6 × 4 = 24

24 ÷ 6 = 4

4 × 8 = 32

32 ÷ 4 = 8

PAGE 60

12 ÷ 4 = 3

18 ÷ 2 = 9

28 ÷ 4 = 7

64 ÷ 8 = 8

21 ÷ 7 = 3

22 ÷ 2 = 11

30 ÷ 6 = 5

50 ÷ 10 = 5

8 ÷ 1 = 8

60 ÷ 6 = 10

10 ÷ 5 = 2

25 ÷ 5 = 5

14 ÷ 2 = 7

40 ÷ 10 = 4

24 ÷ 12 = 2

PAGE 61

12 ÷ 2 = 6

32 ÷ 4 = 8

99 ÷ 11 = 9

35 ÷ 5 = 7

30 ÷ 10 = 3

42 ÷ 6 = 7

7 ÷ 7 = 1

120 ÷ 12 = 10

36 ÷ 9 = 4

18 ÷ 3 = 6

72 ÷ 12 = 6

81 ÷ 9 = 9

54 ÷ 9 = 6

27 ÷ 3 = 9

84 ÷ 12 = 7

110 ÷ 10 = 11

28 ÷ 7 = 4

40 ÷ 8 = 5

PAGE 62

60 ÷ 12 = 5

70 ÷ 10 = 7

20 ÷ 2 = 10

63 ÷ 7 = 9

6 ÷ 1 = 6

45 ÷ 9 = 5

48 ÷ 4 = 12

5 ÷ 5 = 1

8 ÷ 4 = 2

40 ÷ 5 = 8

24 ÷ 3 = 8

84 ÷ 7 = 12

108 ÷ 12 = 9

30 ÷ 5 = 6

22 ÷ 11 = 2

20 ÷ 4 = 5

66 ÷ 6 = 11

36 ÷ 4 = 9

88 ÷ 11 = 8

16 ÷ 2 = 8

110 ÷ 10 = 11

PAGE 63

9 pictures

4 goals

7 cupcakes

4 teams

2 bananas

PAGE 64

1,800 ÷ 2 = 900

21,000 ÷ 3 = 7,000

4,200 ÷ 7 = 600

25,000 ÷ 5 = 5,000

840 ÷ 12 = 70

330 ÷ 11 = 30

36,000 ÷ 6 = 6,000

160 ÷ 4 = 40

2,400 ÷ 3 = 800

40,000 ÷ 8 = 5,000

770 ÷ 7 = 110

PAGE 65

315 ÷ 7 is between 40 and 50.

135 ÷ 9 is between 10 and 20.

264 ÷ 6 is between 40 and 50.

475 ÷ 5 is between 90 and 100.

448 ÷ 8 is between 50 and 60.

234 ÷ 3 is between 70 and 80.

450 ÷ 6 is between 70 and 80.

444 ÷ 12 is between 30 and 40.

PAGE 67

Steps may vary.

162 ÷ 3 = (150 + 12) ÷ 3

162 ÷ 3 = (150 ÷ 3) + (12 ÷ 3)

162 ÷ 3 = 50 + 4

162 ÷ 3 = 54

364 ÷ 7 = (350 + 14) ÷ 7

364 ÷ 7 = (350 ÷ 7) + (14 ÷ 7)

364 ÷ 7 = 50 + 2

364 ÷ 7 = 52

696 ÷ 8 = (640 + 56) ÷ 8

696 ÷ 8 = (640 ÷ 8) + (56 ÷ 8)

696 ÷ 8 = 80 + 7

696 ÷ 8 = 87

PAGE 68

Steps may vary.

152 ÷ 4 = (120 + 32) ÷ 4

152 ÷ 4 = (120 ÷ 4) + (32 ÷ 4)

152 ÷ 4 = 30 + 8

152 ÷ 4 = 38

476 ÷ 7 = (420 + 56) ÷ 7

476 ÷ 7 = (420 ÷ 7) + (56 ÷ 7)

476 ÷ 7 = 60 + 8

476 ÷ 7 = 68

240 ÷ 5 = (200 + 40) ÷ 5

240 ÷ 5 = (200 ÷ 5) + (40 ÷ 5)

240 ÷ 5 = 40 + 8

240 ÷ 5 = 48

PAGE 69

291 ÷ 3 = 97

304 ÷ 4 = 76

318 ÷ 6 = 53

768 ÷ 8 = 96

375 ÷ 5 = 75

581 ÷ 7 = 83

558 ÷ 9 = 62

948 ÷ 12 = 79

PAGE 70

$$3\overline{)63} = 21$$
$$4\overline{)76} = 19$$
$$5\overline{)77} = 15\text{ R2}$$

$$7\overline{)92} = 13\text{ R1}$$
$$6\overline{)98} = 16\text{ R2}$$
$$3\overline{)84} = 28$$

PAGE 71

$$4\overline{)89} = 22\text{ R1}$$
$$3\overline{)81} = 27$$
$$2\overline{)78} = 39$$

$$3\overline{)71} = 23\text{ R2}$$
$$5\overline{)95} = 19$$
$$8\overline{)98} = 12\text{ R2}$$

$$6\overline{)79} = 13\text{ R1}$$
$$7\overline{)99} = 14\text{ R1}$$
$$4\overline{)71} = 17\text{ R3}$$

PAGE 72

$$4\overline{)932} = 233$$
$$2\overline{)656} = 328$$
$$5\overline{)712} = 142\text{ R2}$$

$$3\overline{)521} = 173\text{ R2}$$
$$6\overline{)726} = 121$$
$$8\overline{)894} = 111\text{ R6}$$

$$7\overline{)987} = 141$$
$$4\overline{)949} = 237\text{ R1}$$
$$6\overline{)838} = 139\text{ R4}$$

PAGE 73

$$5\overline{)225} = 45$$
$$2\overline{)818} = 409$$
$$6\overline{)348} = 58$$

$$4\overline{)428} = 107$$
$$8\overline{)632} = 79$$
$$7\overline{)756} = 108$$

PAGE 74

$$5\overline{)544} = 108\text{ R4}$$
$$4\overline{)688} = 172$$
$$3\overline{)228} = 76$$

$$6\overline{)630} = 105$$
$$7\overline{)905} = 129\text{ R2}$$
$$9\overline{)752} = 83\text{ R5}$$

$$4\overline{)733} = 183\text{ R1}$$
$$6\overline{)564} = 94$$
$$8\overline{)997} = 124\text{ R5}$$

PAGE 75

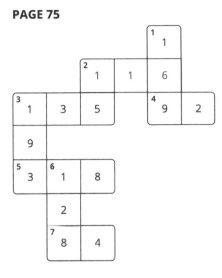

PAGE 76

$$4\overline{)1,385} = 346\text{ R1}$$
$$7\overline{)2,969} = 424\text{ R1}$$
$$2\overline{)4,250} = 2,125$$

$$5\overline{)6,347} = 1,269\text{ R2}$$
$$9\overline{)8,262} = 918$$
$$8\overline{)7,279} = 909\text{ R7}$$

$$5\overline{)4,630} = 926$$
$$6\overline{)8,004} = 1,334$$
$$2\overline{)9,307} = 4,653\text{ R1}$$

PAGE 77

34 flower arrangements with 4 flowers left over

44 days with 2 cups of dog food left over

90 treat bags with 5 pieces of candy left over

6 seeds

PAGE 78

24 cabins

34 packages

71 orders

20 tours

359 boxes

PAGE 79

14   (28)   (44)   49

(12)   16   (24)   (54)

17   23   (28)   (42)

29   (36)   (45)   (72)

(546)   251   (722)   863

PAGE 79, *continued*

20 and 45 are both divisible by 5.

12 and 27 are both divisible by 3.

21 and 49 are both divisible by 7.

PAGE 80

12: 1, 2, 3, 4, 6, 12

9: 1, 3, 9

13: 1, 13

18: 1, 2, 3, 6, 9, 18

24: 1, 2, 3, 4, 6, 8, 12, 24

22: 1, 2, 11, 22

20: 1, 2, 4, 5, 10, 20

23: 1, 23

27: 1, 3, 9, 27

49: 1, 7, 49

PAGE 81

4: 4, 8, 12, 16

6: 6, 12, 18, 24

7: 7, 14, 21, 28

9: 9, 18, 27, 36

10: 10, 20, 30, 40

12: 12, 24, 36, 48

15: 15, 30, 45, 60

30: 30, 60, 90, 120

80: 80, 160, 240, 320

112: 112, 224, 336, 448

205: 205, 410, 615, 820

PAGE 82

START				FINISH
6 is a factor of 18.	6 is a multiple of 18.	32 is divisible by 6.	21 is divisible by 7.	14 is a multiple of 2.
27 is a multiple of 3.	24 is divisible by 5.	4 is a factor of 40.	5 is a factor of 30.	4 is a multiple of 12.
16 is a multiple of 2.	35 is a factor of 7.	48 is divisible by 8.	6 is a multiple of 12.	9 is a factor of 24.
20 is divisible by 5.	7 is a factor of 28.	36 is a multiple of 9.	8 is divisible by 32.	18 is a multiple of 4.

Answer key

PAGE 83

6: 1, 2, 3, 6	Composite
11: 1, 11	Prime
4: 1, 2, 4	Composite
16 : 1, 2, 4, 8, 16	Composite
19: 1, 19	Prime
35: 1, 5, 7, 35	Composite
23: 1, 23	Prime

PAGE 84

② ③ 4̸ ⑤ 6̸ ⑦ 8̸ 9̸ 1̸0̸
⑪ 1̸2̸ ⑬ 1̸4̸ 1̸5̸ 1̸6̸ ⑰ 1̸8̸ ⑲ 2̸0̸
2̸1̸ 2̸2̸ ㉓ 2̸4̸ 2̸5̸ 2̸6̸ 2̸7̸ 2̸8̸ ㉙ 3̸0̸
㉛ 3̸2̸ 3̸3̸ 3̸4̸ 3̸5̸ 3̸6̸ �37 3̸8̸ 3̸9̸ 4̸0̸
㊶ 4̸2̸ ㊸ 4̸4̸ 4̸5̸ 4̸6̸ ㊼ 4̸8̸ 4̸9̸ 5̸0̸
5̸1̸ 5̸2̸ ㊾ 5̸4̸ 5̸5̸ 5̸6̸ 5̸7̸ 5̸8̸ ㊾ 6̸0̸

PAGE 85

Answers may vary. Some possible answers are shown below.

6 = 3 + 3   18 = 13 + 5
32 = 29 + 3   40 = 17 + 23

17 = 5 + 5 + 7   33 = 3 + 13 + 17
41 = 17 + 13 + 11   59 = 29 + 23 + 7

PAGE 86

225	300	375	450	525

745	645	545	445	345

2,340	2,590	2,840	3,090	3,340

5,934	5,534	5,134	4,734	4,334

7,026	7,746	8,466	9,186	9,906

PAGE 87

add 45

577	622	667	712	757

subtract 115

1,150	1,035	920	805	690

PAGE 87, *continued*

subtract 360

2,075	1,715	1,355	995	635

add 460

3,040	3,500	3,960	4,420	4,880

subtract 520

8,900	8,380	7,860	7,340	6,820

PAGE 88

6	18	54	162	486

192	96	48	24	12

6	30	150	750	3,750

4,802	686	98	14	2

6	36	216	1,296	7,776

2,048	512	128	32	8

PAGE 89

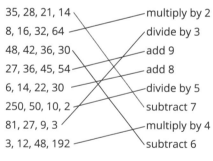

35, 28, 21, 14 — multiply by 2
8, 16, 32, 64 — divide by 3
48, 42, 36, 30 — add 9
27, 36, 45, 54 — add 8
6, 14, 22, 30 — divide by 5
250, 50, 10, 2 — subtract 7
81, 27, 9, 3 — multiply by 4
3, 12, 48, 192 — subtract 6

The next three numbers for the last sequence are 768, 3,072, and 12,288.

PAGE 90

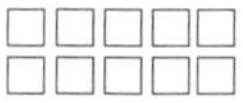

Figure 4

Figure 4

PAGE 91

Figure	Number of lines
1	3
2	5
3	7
4	9
5	11
6	13

Figure	Number of squares
1	1
2	3
3	6
4	10
5	15
6	21

PAGE 92

The next term is found by adding the two terms before it.

89, 144, 233, 377, 610, 987

PAGE 93

$\frac{1}{4}$ $\frac{1}{2}$ $\frac{2}{5}$

$\frac{5}{8}$ $\frac{4}{6}$ $\frac{3}{8}$

PAGE 94

$\frac{3}{5}$ $\frac{2}{3}$

$\frac{4}{12}$ $\frac{2}{5}$

PAGE 95

$\frac{3}{5}$

$\frac{1}{4}$

$\frac{5}{8}$

PAGE 96

Shading may vary. Some possible answers are shown below.

PAGE 97

PAGE 98

$$\frac{3}{4} = \frac{6}{8} \qquad \frac{1}{2} = \frac{4}{8}$$

$$\frac{2}{8} = \frac{1}{4} \qquad \frac{1}{3} = \frac{3}{9}$$

$$\frac{2}{5} = \frac{4}{10}$$

PAGE 99

$$\frac{3}{5} = \frac{6}{10}$$

$$\frac{1}{4} = \frac{2}{8}$$

$$\frac{4}{6} = \frac{2}{3}$$

PAGE 100

$$\frac{4}{6} = \frac{8}{12} \qquad \frac{4}{5} = \frac{12}{15} \qquad \frac{3}{4} = \frac{6}{8}$$

$$\frac{6}{8} = \frac{18}{24} \qquad \frac{1}{2} = \frac{8}{16} \qquad \frac{2}{3} = \frac{10}{15}$$

$$\frac{3}{5} = \frac{12}{20} \qquad \frac{2}{6} = \frac{6}{18} \qquad \frac{1}{3} = \frac{7}{21}$$

PAGE 101

$$\frac{3}{9} = \frac{1}{3} \qquad \frac{6}{10} = \frac{3}{5} \qquad \frac{8}{12} = \frac{2}{3}$$

$$\frac{9}{12} = \frac{3}{4} \qquad \frac{4}{16} = \frac{1}{4} \qquad \frac{3}{15} = \frac{1}{5}$$

$$\frac{8}{20} = \frac{2}{5} \qquad \frac{15}{25} = \frac{3}{5}$$

PAGE 102

$$\frac{12}{16} = \frac{3}{4} \qquad \frac{4}{10} = \frac{2}{5}$$

$$\frac{10}{15} = \frac{2}{3} \qquad \frac{6}{9} = \frac{2}{3}$$

$$\frac{4}{14} = \frac{2}{7} \qquad \frac{12}{20} = \frac{3}{5}$$

$$\frac{20}{24} = \frac{5}{6} \qquad \frac{14}{28} = \frac{1}{2}$$

PAGE 103

no, $\frac{1}{2}$ yes

no, $\frac{1}{3}$ no, $\frac{5}{12}$

yes   no, $\frac{1}{2}$

no, $\frac{1}{4}$ yes

yes   no, $\frac{2}{5}$

no, $\frac{1}{5}$ no, $\frac{2}{3}$

PAGE 104

$$\frac{3}{4} > \frac{2}{4} \qquad \frac{1}{3} < \frac{2}{3}$$

$$\frac{5}{6} > \frac{4}{6} \qquad \frac{7}{12} > \frac{6}{12}$$

$$\frac{5}{8} > \frac{3}{8} \qquad \frac{8}{9} = \frac{8}{9}$$

$$\frac{4}{10} < \frac{8}{10} \qquad \frac{1}{7} < \frac{3}{7}$$

PAGE 105

$$\frac{1}{4} > \frac{1}{10} \qquad \frac{1}{3} > \frac{1}{5}$$

$$\frac{1}{12} < \frac{1}{6} \qquad \frac{1}{8} < \frac{1}{3}$$

$$\frac{1}{5} > \frac{1}{6} \qquad \frac{1}{7} > \frac{1}{9} \qquad \frac{1}{8} < \frac{1}{2}$$

PAGE 106

$$\frac{5}{8} > \frac{5}{10} \qquad \frac{2}{3} > \frac{2}{5}$$

$$\frac{4}{9} < \frac{4}{6} \qquad \frac{7}{8} > \frac{7}{12}$$

$$\frac{6}{12} = \frac{6}{12} \qquad \frac{3}{5} < \frac{3}{4}$$

$$\frac{2}{7} < \frac{4}{5} \qquad \frac{4}{6} > \frac{3}{10} \qquad \frac{3}{4} > \frac{2}{5}$$

PAGE 107

$$\frac{4}{5} > \frac{3}{5} \qquad \frac{1}{9} < \frac{1}{5} \qquad \frac{3}{6} > \frac{3}{8}$$

$$\frac{1}{4} < \frac{1}{3} \qquad \frac{6}{8} < \frac{7}{8} \qquad \frac{4}{5} > \frac{4}{8}$$

$$\frac{10}{11} > \frac{10}{12} \qquad \frac{3}{12} > \frac{2}{12} \qquad \frac{7}{9} < \frac{8}{9}$$

$$\frac{14}{15} > \frac{13}{15} \qquad \frac{12}{16} < \frac{12}{15} \qquad \frac{20}{25} > \frac{20}{30}$$

PAGE 108

$$\frac{2}{6} < \frac{1}{2}$$

$$\frac{5}{8} > \frac{1}{2}$$

Answer key

PAGE 109

$\frac{2}{8} < \frac{1}{2}$ $\frac{5}{6} > \frac{1}{2}$ $\frac{4}{5} > \frac{1}{2}$

$\frac{2}{4} = \frac{1}{2}$ $\frac{1}{6} < \frac{1}{2}$ $\frac{7}{10} > \frac{1}{2}$

$\frac{3}{8} < \frac{1}{2}$ $\frac{6}{12} = \frac{1}{2}$ $\frac{4}{9} < \frac{1}{2}$

$\frac{2}{5} < \frac{1}{2}$ $\frac{4}{7} > \frac{1}{2}$ $\frac{4}{8} = \frac{1}{2}$

PAGE 110

$\frac{1}{3} < \frac{3}{4}$ $\frac{7}{12} > \frac{2}{5}$ $\frac{2}{6} < \frac{8}{10}$

$\frac{2}{8} < \frac{3}{5}$ $\frac{3}{8} < \frac{4}{7}$ $\frac{5}{10} = \frac{3}{6}$

$\frac{2}{6} < \frac{4}{8}$ $\frac{2}{3} > \frac{4}{12}$ $\frac{5}{11} < \frac{7}{8}$

$\frac{4}{7} > \frac{2}{6}$ $\frac{5}{10} < \frac{6}{9}$ $\frac{1}{3} < \frac{3}{5}$

PAGE 111

$\frac{3}{4} > \frac{7}{12}$ $\frac{1}{5} < \frac{3}{10}$

$\frac{2}{3} > \frac{5}{9}$ $\frac{5}{8} < \frac{3}{4}$

$\frac{4}{6} = \frac{2}{3}$ $\frac{1}{3} < \frac{5}{12}$

$\frac{1}{3} > \frac{2}{9}$ $\frac{3}{4} > \frac{8}{12}$

PAGE 112

LCM: 12   LCM: 21

$\frac{8}{12} < \frac{9}{12}$ $\frac{7}{21} > \frac{6}{21}$

LCM: 18   LCM: 6

$\frac{14}{18} > \frac{12}{18}$ $\frac{4}{6} < \frac{5}{6}$

PAGE 113

LCM: 12   LCM: 24

$\frac{3}{12} < \frac{4}{12}$ $\frac{16}{24} < \frac{18}{24}$

LCM: 20   LCM: 35

$\frac{6}{20} > \frac{5}{20}$ $\frac{14}{35} < \frac{15}{35}$

LCM: 28   LCM: 36

$\frac{21}{28} > \frac{20}{28}$ $\frac{24}{36} = \frac{24}{36}$

PAGE 113, *continued*

LCM: 40   LCM: 24

$\frac{10}{40} < \frac{12}{40}$ $\frac{15}{24} > \frac{14}{24}$

PAGE 114

$\frac{3}{4} > \frac{5}{8}$ $\frac{2}{5} > \frac{3}{10}$ $\frac{2}{6} = \frac{1}{3}$

$\frac{2}{6} < \frac{5}{12}$ $\frac{4}{9} > \frac{1}{3}$ $\frac{1}{3} > \frac{3}{12}$

$\frac{1}{4} = \frac{3}{12}$ $\frac{2}{8} < \frac{1}{3}$ $\frac{3}{4} > \frac{4}{6}$

$\frac{7}{10} < \frac{3}{4}$ $\frac{5}{7} > \frac{2}{3}$ $\frac{3}{5} < \frac{4}{6}$

Answers may vary. Some possible answers are shown below.

$\frac{5}{8} > \frac{3}{8}$ $\frac{4}{5} > \frac{6}{12}$ $\frac{2}{5} < \frac{6}{8}$

PAGE 115

| $\frac{1}{5}$ | $\frac{1}{3}$ | $\frac{2}{3}$ |

| $\frac{4}{10}$ | $\frac{6}{10}$ | $\frac{4}{5}$ |

| $\frac{2}{12}$ | $\frac{2}{5}$ | $\frac{5}{6}$ |

| $\frac{1}{4}$ | $\frac{3}{10}$ | $\frac{2}{5}$ |

| $\frac{2}{3}$ | $\frac{3}{4}$ | $\frac{5}{6}$ |

| $\frac{4}{12}$ | $\frac{1}{2}$ | $\frac{5}{8}$ | $\frac{3}{4}$ |

| $\frac{1}{4}$ | $\frac{2}{6}$ | $\frac{5}{12}$ | $\frac{2}{3}$ |

PAGE 116

more

the post office

Robin

red leashes

the blue piece of yarn

PAGE 117

$\frac{4}{5} = \frac{1}{5} + \frac{1}{5} + \frac{1}{5} + \frac{1}{5}$

$\frac{5}{8} = \frac{1}{8} + \frac{1}{8} + \frac{1}{8} + \frac{1}{8} + \frac{1}{8}$

$\frac{2}{3} = \frac{1}{3} + \frac{1}{3}$

$\frac{3}{9} = \frac{1}{9} + \frac{1}{9} + \frac{1}{9}$

$\frac{4}{6} = \frac{1}{6} + \frac{1}{6} + \frac{1}{6} + \frac{1}{6}$

$\frac{3}{10} = \frac{1}{10} + \frac{1}{10} + \frac{1}{10}$

$\frac{2}{4} = \frac{1}{4} + \frac{1}{4}$

$\frac{5}{12} = \frac{1}{12} + \frac{1}{12} + \frac{1}{12} + \frac{1}{12} + \frac{1}{12}$

Fractions can be written in lots of equivalent ways! For the next few pages, this answer key will include both the answer your child is most likely to write down and its simplest form.

PAGE 118

Placement of shading may vary. Some possible answers are shown below.

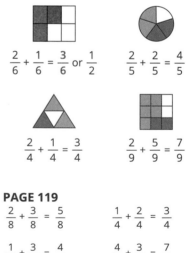

$\frac{2}{6} + \frac{1}{6} = \frac{3}{6}$ or $\frac{1}{2}$ $\frac{2}{5} + \frac{2}{5} = \frac{4}{5}$

$\frac{2}{4} + \frac{1}{4} = \frac{3}{4}$ $\frac{2}{9} + \frac{5}{9} = \frac{7}{9}$

PAGE 119

$\frac{2}{8} + \frac{3}{8} = \frac{5}{8}$ $\frac{1}{4} + \frac{2}{4} = \frac{3}{4}$

$\frac{1}{5} + \frac{3}{5} = \frac{4}{5}$ $\frac{4}{8} + \frac{3}{8} = \frac{7}{8}$

$\frac{5}{9} + \frac{3}{9} = \frac{8}{9}$ $\frac{1}{6} + \frac{4}{6} = \frac{5}{6}$

$\frac{4}{10} + \frac{4}{10} = \frac{8}{10}$ or $\frac{4}{5}$ $\frac{3}{7} + \frac{2}{7} = \frac{5}{7}$

$\frac{4}{11} + \frac{5}{11} = \frac{9}{11}$ $\frac{1}{5} + \frac{2}{5} = \frac{3}{5}$

$\frac{7}{12} + \frac{4}{12} = \frac{11}{12}$

PAGE 120

Placement of shading may vary. Some possible answers are shown below.

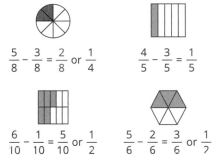

$\dfrac{5}{8} - \dfrac{3}{8} = \dfrac{2}{8}$ or $\dfrac{1}{4}$ $\dfrac{4}{5} - \dfrac{3}{5} = \dfrac{1}{5}$

$\dfrac{6}{10} - \dfrac{1}{10} = \dfrac{5}{10}$ or $\dfrac{1}{2}$ $\dfrac{5}{6} - \dfrac{2}{6} = \dfrac{3}{6}$ or $\dfrac{1}{2}$

PAGE 121

$\dfrac{2}{3} - \dfrac{1}{3} = \dfrac{1}{3}$ $\dfrac{6}{8} - \dfrac{2}{8} = \dfrac{4}{8}$ or $\dfrac{1}{2}$

$\dfrac{4}{5} - \dfrac{2}{5} = \dfrac{2}{5}$ $\dfrac{3}{4} - \dfrac{2}{4} = \dfrac{1}{4}$

$\dfrac{3}{6} - \dfrac{1}{6} = \dfrac{2}{6}$ or $\dfrac{1}{3}$ $\dfrac{8}{10} - \dfrac{3}{10} = \dfrac{5}{10}$ or $\dfrac{1}{2}$

$\dfrac{4}{7} - \dfrac{2}{7} = \dfrac{2}{7}$ $\dfrac{7}{9} - \dfrac{2}{9} = \dfrac{5}{9}$

$\dfrac{10}{12} - \dfrac{4}{12} = \dfrac{6}{12}$ or $\dfrac{1}{2}$ $\dfrac{4}{8} - \dfrac{1}{8} = \dfrac{3}{8}$

$\dfrac{9}{11} - \dfrac{2}{11} = \dfrac{7}{11}$

PAGE 122

$\dfrac{2}{6} + \dfrac{3}{6} = \dfrac{5}{6}$ $\dfrac{7}{8} - \dfrac{4}{8} = \dfrac{3}{8}$

$\dfrac{4}{5} - \dfrac{2}{5} = \dfrac{2}{5}$ $\dfrac{3}{7} + \dfrac{1}{7} = \dfrac{4}{7}$

$\dfrac{5}{6} - \dfrac{3}{6} = \dfrac{2}{6}$ or $\dfrac{1}{3}$ $\dfrac{9}{10} - \dfrac{2}{10} = \dfrac{7}{10}$

$\dfrac{2}{9} + \dfrac{4}{9} = \dfrac{6}{9}$ or $\dfrac{2}{3}$ $\dfrac{2}{11} + \dfrac{6}{11} = \dfrac{8}{11}$

$\dfrac{5}{7} - \dfrac{3}{7} = \dfrac{2}{7}$ $\dfrac{3}{8} + \dfrac{3}{8} = \dfrac{6}{8}$ or $\dfrac{3}{4}$

$\dfrac{5}{10} + \dfrac{3}{10} = \dfrac{8}{10}$ or $\dfrac{4}{5}$ $\dfrac{9}{12} - \dfrac{5}{12} = \dfrac{4}{12}$ or $\dfrac{1}{3}$

PAGE 123

$\dfrac{2}{8}$ or $\dfrac{1}{4}$ of a quart

$\dfrac{7}{12}$ of the hot-air balloons

$\dfrac{5}{8}$ of the pizza

$\dfrac{3}{4}$ of a cup

PAGE 123, *continued*

$\dfrac{2}{5}$ of the bottle

PAGE 124

$3\dfrac{2}{3}$

$1\dfrac{4}{5}$

$2\dfrac{2}{4}$ or $2\dfrac{1}{2}$

$1\dfrac{5}{8}$

PAGE 125

Drawings may vary. Some possible answers are shown below.

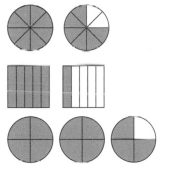

PAGE 126

$\dfrac{16}{6}$ or $\dfrac{8}{3}$

$\dfrac{18}{10}$ or $\dfrac{9}{5}$

$\dfrac{7}{2}$

$\dfrac{8}{3}$

PAGE 127

Drawings may vary. Some possible answers are shown below.

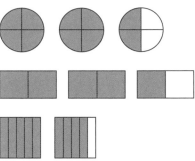

PAGE 128

$\dfrac{6}{2} = 3$

$\dfrac{11}{4} = 2\dfrac{3}{4}$

$\dfrac{23}{6} = 3\dfrac{5}{6}$

$\dfrac{16}{8} = 2$

PAGE 129

$\dfrac{11}{3} = 3\dfrac{2}{3}$ $\dfrac{7}{4} = 1\dfrac{3}{4}$

$\dfrac{14}{6} = 2\dfrac{2}{6}$ or $2\dfrac{1}{3}$ $\dfrac{27}{9} = 3$

$\dfrac{17}{12} = 1\dfrac{5}{12}$ $\dfrac{25}{8} = 3\dfrac{1}{8}$

$2\dfrac{2}{5} = \dfrac{12}{5}$ $2\dfrac{3}{8} = \dfrac{19}{8}$

$4\dfrac{1}{2} = \dfrac{9}{2}$ $2\dfrac{3}{7} = \dfrac{17}{7}$

$3\dfrac{3}{10} = \dfrac{33}{10}$ $3\dfrac{5}{11} = \dfrac{38}{11}$

PAGE 130

$4\dfrac{1}{3} + 6\dfrac{1}{3} = 10\dfrac{2}{3}$

$5\dfrac{2}{6} + 2\dfrac{3}{6} = 7\dfrac{5}{6}$

$7\dfrac{4}{8} + 3\dfrac{2}{8} = 10\dfrac{6}{8}$ or $10\dfrac{3}{4}$

PAGE 130, *continued*

$4\frac{3}{9} + 9\frac{4}{9} = 13\frac{7}{9}$

$2\frac{3}{10} + 11\frac{5}{10} = 13\frac{8}{10}$ or $13\frac{4}{5}$

$13\frac{5}{12} + 5\frac{5}{12} = 18\frac{10}{12}$ or $18\frac{5}{6}$

PAGE 131

$9\frac{1}{4} + 4\frac{1}{4} = 13\frac{2}{4}$ or $13\frac{1}{2}$

$11\frac{3}{7} + 7\frac{1}{7} = 18\frac{4}{7}$

$8\frac{1}{5} + 8\frac{1}{5} = 16\frac{2}{5}$

$14\frac{3}{8} + 12\frac{2}{8} = 26\frac{5}{8}$

$8\frac{2}{9} + 12\frac{5}{9} = 20\frac{7}{9}$

$22\frac{2}{6} + 6\frac{2}{6} = 28\frac{4}{6}$ or $28\frac{2}{3}$

$27\frac{3}{10} + 10\frac{5}{10} = 37\frac{8}{10}$ or $37\frac{4}{5}$

$9\frac{2}{12} + 16\frac{7}{12} = 25\frac{9}{12}$ or $25\frac{3}{4}$

$24\frac{5}{11} + 19\frac{5}{11} = 43\frac{10}{11}$

$13\frac{3}{8} + 18\frac{1}{8} = 31\frac{4}{8}$ or $31\frac{1}{2}$

PAGE 132

$4\frac{2}{3} + 2\frac{2}{3} = 7\frac{1}{3}$

$3\frac{3}{5} + 5\frac{4}{5} = 9\frac{2}{5}$

$6\frac{4}{8} + 3\frac{6}{8} = 10\frac{2}{8}$ or $10\frac{1}{4}$

$2\frac{2}{4} + 8\frac{3}{4} = 11\frac{1}{4}$

$12\frac{6}{9} + 6\frac{5}{9} = 19\frac{2}{9}$

$10\frac{7}{12} + 7\frac{9}{12} = 18\frac{4}{12}$ or $18\frac{1}{3}$

PAGE 133

$12\frac{7}{8} + 4\frac{3}{8} = 17\frac{2}{8}$ or $17\frac{1}{4}$

$2\frac{9}{10} + 17\frac{7}{10} = 20\frac{6}{10}$ or $20\frac{3}{5}$

$13\frac{5}{7} + 13\frac{5}{7} = 27\frac{3}{7}$

$16\frac{3}{6} + 23\frac{5}{6} = 40\frac{2}{6}$ or $40\frac{1}{3}$

$16\frac{4}{5} + 22\frac{4}{5} = 39\frac{3}{5}$

$21\frac{4}{11} + 14\frac{7}{11} = 36$

$15\frac{7}{9} + 28\frac{8}{9} = 44\frac{6}{9}$ or $44\frac{2}{3}$

$17\frac{8}{12} + 11\frac{8}{12} = 29\frac{4}{12}$ or $29\frac{1}{3}$

$23\frac{7}{10} + 7\frac{3}{10} = 31$

$25\frac{5}{7} + 2\frac{6}{7} = 28\frac{4}{7}$

$17\frac{9}{11} + 29\frac{5}{11} = 47\frac{3}{11}$

$37\frac{10}{12} + 17\frac{7}{12} = 55\frac{5}{12}$

PAGE 134

$3\frac{4}{5} + 3\frac{3}{5} = 7\frac{2}{5}$

$2\frac{3}{6} + 4\frac{2}{6} = 6\frac{5}{6}$

$5\frac{1}{4} + 7\frac{2}{4} = 12\frac{3}{4}$

$9\frac{2}{3} + 3\frac{2}{3} = 13\frac{1}{3}$

$4\frac{6}{10} + 4\frac{7}{10} = 9\frac{3}{10}$

$6\frac{5}{8} + 7\frac{4}{8} = 14\frac{1}{8}$

$3\frac{2}{7} + 10\frac{3}{7} = 13\frac{5}{7}$

$4\frac{4}{12} + 3\frac{3}{12} = 7\frac{7}{12}$

$5\frac{3}{9} + 5\frac{8}{9} = 11\frac{2}{9}$

$13\frac{4}{5} + 4\frac{2}{5} = 18\frac{1}{5}$

PAGE 135

$5\frac{2}{3} - 1\frac{1}{3} = 4\frac{1}{3}$

$8\frac{4}{5} - 5\frac{2}{5} = 3\frac{2}{5}$

$7\frac{7}{8} - 2\frac{3}{8} = 5\frac{4}{8}$ or $5\frac{1}{2}$

$15\frac{2}{4} - 7\frac{1}{4} = 8\frac{1}{4}$

$16\frac{8}{12} - 8\frac{3}{12} = 8\frac{5}{12}$

$19\frac{7}{9} - 12\frac{3}{9} = 7\frac{4}{9}$

PAGE 136

$16\frac{3}{5} - 3\frac{2}{5} = 13\frac{1}{5}$

$10\frac{3}{8} - 7\frac{1}{8} = 3\frac{2}{8}$ or $3\frac{1}{4}$

$12\frac{3}{4} - 6\frac{1}{4} = 6\frac{2}{4}$ or $6\frac{1}{2}$

$18\frac{5}{6} - 10\frac{5}{6} = 8$

$17\frac{5}{12} - 6\frac{3}{12} = 11\frac{2}{12}$ or $11\frac{1}{6}$

$19\frac{8}{9} - 12\frac{6}{9} = 7\frac{2}{9}$

$21\frac{4}{5} - 13\frac{1}{5} = 8\frac{3}{5}$

$20\frac{5}{7} - 15\frac{3}{7} = 5\frac{2}{7}$

$27\frac{9}{12} - 8\frac{7}{12} = 19\frac{2}{12}$ or $19\frac{1}{6}$

$15\frac{5}{8} - 14\frac{4}{8} = 1\frac{1}{8}$

PAGE 137

$8\frac{3}{8} - 3\frac{5}{8} = 4\frac{6}{8}$ or $4\frac{3}{4}$

$5\frac{3}{6} - 2\frac{5}{6} = 2\frac{4}{6}$ or $2\frac{2}{3}$

$7\frac{2}{5} - 5\frac{4}{5} = 1\frac{3}{5}$

$14\frac{4}{9} - 8\frac{7}{9} = 5\frac{6}{9}$ or $5\frac{2}{3}$

PAGE 138

$7 - 3\frac{7}{8} = 3\frac{1}{8}$

$8\frac{1}{4} - 1\frac{3}{4} = 6\frac{2}{4}$ or $6\frac{1}{2}$

$11\frac{4}{6} - 2\frac{5}{6} = 8\frac{5}{6}$

$15\frac{2}{10} - 12\frac{7}{10} = 2\frac{5}{10}$ or $2\frac{1}{2}$

$16 - 6\frac{5}{8} = 9\frac{3}{8}$

$19\frac{7}{12} - 10\frac{9}{12} = 8\frac{10}{12}$ or $8\frac{5}{6}$

$12\frac{3}{9} - 7\frac{8}{9} = 4\frac{4}{9}$

$10\frac{1}{7} - 4\frac{2}{7} = 5\frac{6}{7}$

$17\frac{6}{11} - 3\frac{10}{11} = 13\frac{7}{11}$

$24 - 19\frac{5}{6} = 4\frac{1}{6}$

$27\frac{2}{12} - 18\frac{6}{12} = 8\frac{8}{12}$ or $8\frac{2}{3}$

$15\frac{4}{9} - 7\frac{7}{9} = 7\frac{6}{9}$ or $7\frac{2}{3}$

PAGE 139

$10\frac{1}{5} - 4\frac{3}{5} = 5\frac{3}{5}$

$5\frac{1}{4} - 1\frac{3}{4} = 3\frac{2}{4}$ or $3\frac{1}{2}$

$6\frac{5}{6} - 2\frac{3}{6} = 4\frac{2}{6}$ or $4\frac{1}{3}$

$8\frac{4}{5} - 4\frac{2}{5} = 4\frac{2}{5}$

$10\frac{3}{9} - 4\frac{5}{9} = 5\frac{7}{9}$

$12\frac{7}{12} - 7\frac{4}{12} = 5\frac{3}{12}$ or $5\frac{1}{4}$

$9 - 2\frac{4}{6} = 6\frac{2}{6}$ or $6\frac{1}{3}$

$15\frac{4}{10} - 7\frac{5}{10} = 7\frac{9}{10}$

$18\frac{3}{7} - 12\frac{1}{7} = 6\frac{2}{7}$

$13 - 9\frac{2}{3} = 3\frac{1}{3}$

PAGE 140

$10\frac{5}{8} - 6\frac{4}{8} = 4\frac{1}{8}$

$13\frac{5}{6} + 12\frac{5}{6} = 26\frac{4}{6}$ or $26\frac{2}{3}$

$19\frac{2}{9} + 11\frac{5}{9} = 30\frac{7}{9}$

$8\frac{2}{5} - 7\frac{3}{5} = \frac{4}{5}$

$5\frac{5}{7} + 16\frac{2}{7} = 22$

$14\frac{9}{12} + 6\frac{1}{12} = 20\frac{10}{12}$ or $20\frac{5}{6}$

$9\frac{8}{9} - 2\frac{4}{9} = 7\frac{4}{9}$

$14\frac{5}{10} - 8\frac{9}{10} = 5\frac{6}{10}$ or $5\frac{3}{5}$

$19\frac{7}{11} + 17\frac{9}{11} = 37\frac{5}{11}$

$13 - 8\frac{1}{4} = 4\frac{3}{4}$

$25\frac{4}{7} + 15\frac{6}{7} = 41\frac{3}{7}$

PAGE 141

$12\frac{1}{8}$ pounds

$1\frac{10}{12}$ or $1\frac{5}{6}$ feet

21 cups

$\frac{2}{3}$ of an hour

$10\frac{6}{8}$ or $10\frac{3}{4}$ pizzas

PAGE 142

$3 \times \frac{1}{4} = \frac{3}{4}$

$2 \times \frac{2}{6} = \frac{4}{6}$ or $\frac{2}{3}$

$3 \times \frac{3}{10} = \frac{9}{10}$

$4 \times \frac{2}{9} = \frac{8}{9}$

PAGE 143

$4 \times \frac{4}{5} = \frac{16}{5}$

$5 \times \frac{3}{8} = \frac{15}{8}$

$3 \times \frac{2}{4} = \frac{6}{4}$ or $\frac{3}{2}$

$5 \times \frac{4}{6} = \frac{20}{6}$ or $\frac{10}{3}$

$2 \times \frac{2}{3} = \frac{4}{3}$

PAGE 144

$3 \times \frac{2}{8} = \frac{6}{8}$ or $\frac{3}{4}$

$4 \times \frac{3}{5} = \frac{12}{5}$

$4 \times \frac{3}{4} = \frac{12}{4}$ or $\frac{3}{1}$

$5 \times \frac{6}{9} = \frac{30}{9}$ or $\frac{10}{3}$

$3 \times \frac{4}{10} = \frac{12}{10}$ or $\frac{6}{5}$

PAGE 145

$6 \times \frac{3}{5} = \frac{18}{5}$

$7 \times \frac{1}{4} = \frac{7}{4}$

$6 \times \frac{2}{11} = \frac{12}{11}$

$9 \times \frac{3}{10} = \frac{27}{10}$

$7 \times \frac{4}{6} = \frac{28}{6}$ or $\frac{14}{3}$

$4 \times \frac{2}{8} = \frac{8}{8}$ or $\frac{1}{1}$

$3 \times \frac{4}{5} = \frac{12}{5}$

$8 \times \frac{4}{9} = \frac{32}{9}$

$7 \times \frac{3}{7} = \frac{21}{7}$ or $\frac{3}{1}$

$11 \times \frac{2}{10} = \frac{22}{10}$ or $\frac{11}{5}$

PAGE 146

$5 \times \frac{2}{3} = \frac{10}{3}$

$3 \times \frac{4}{7} = \frac{12}{7}$

$5 \times \frac{3}{4} = \frac{15}{4}$

$11 \times \frac{2}{7} = \frac{22}{7}$

$7 \times \frac{7}{10} = \frac{49}{10}$

$4 \times \frac{5}{11} = \frac{20}{11}$

$2 \times \frac{7}{9} = \frac{14}{9}$

$7 \times \frac{5}{8} = \frac{35}{8}$

$8 \times \frac{5}{8} = \frac{40}{8}$ or $\frac{5}{1}$

$5 \times \frac{5}{12} = \frac{25}{12}$

$10 \times \frac{2}{9} = \frac{20}{9}$

$8 \times \frac{4}{7} = \frac{32}{7}$

PAGE 146, *continued*

$3\frac{1}{3}$ $1\frac{5}{9}$

$1\frac{5}{7}$ $4\frac{3}{8}$

$3\frac{3}{4}$ 5

$3\frac{1}{7}$ $2\frac{1}{12}$

$4\frac{9}{10}$ $2\frac{2}{9}$

$1\frac{9}{11}$ $4\frac{4}{7}$

PAGE 147

$\frac{16}{5} > \frac{12}{5}$ $\frac{6}{4} > \frac{3}{4}$

$\frac{28}{6} > \frac{25}{6}$ $\frac{9}{8} < \frac{30}{8}$

$\frac{18}{10} = \frac{18}{10}$ $\frac{35}{7} > \frac{32}{7}$

$\frac{56}{9} > \frac{48}{9}$ $\frac{72}{12} > \frac{42}{12}$

PAGE 148

$\frac{5}{8}$ of a cup

$\frac{3}{5}$ of a mile

$1\frac{2}{4}$ or $1\frac{1}{2}$ cups

$\frac{2}{1}$ or 2 tablespoons

PAGE 149

$4\frac{3}{8} + 2\frac{7}{8} = 7\frac{2}{8}$ or $7\frac{1}{4}$

$\frac{7}{10} - \frac{3}{10} = \frac{4}{10}$ or $\frac{2}{5}$

$3 \times \frac{4}{6} = \frac{12}{6}$ or $\frac{2}{1}$

$4\frac{2}{3} + \frac{2}{3} = 5\frac{1}{3}$

$5\frac{3}{4} - 2\frac{1}{4} = 3\frac{2}{4}$ or $3\frac{1}{2}$

$7 \times \frac{2}{8} = \frac{14}{8}$ or $\frac{7}{4}$

PAGE 149, *continued*

$7\frac{5}{7} + 4\frac{4}{7} = 12\frac{2}{7}$

$6\frac{1}{2} - 1\frac{1}{2} = 5$

$9 \times \frac{5}{12} = \frac{45}{12}$ or $\frac{15}{4}$

$8\frac{2}{3} + 5\frac{1}{3} = 14$

$12\frac{3}{10} - 4\frac{7}{10} = 7\frac{6}{10}$ or $7\frac{3}{5}$

$8 \times \frac{4}{7} = \frac{32}{7}$

PAGE 150

$9 \times \frac{9}{10} = \frac{81}{10}$

$4\frac{2}{3} + 6\frac{1}{3} = 11$

$18\frac{3}{5} - 2\frac{2}{5} = 16\frac{1}{5}$

$8 \times \frac{8}{9} = \frac{64}{9}$

$13\frac{1}{7} - 10\frac{5}{7} = 2\frac{3}{7}$

$17\frac{4}{6} + 11\frac{4}{6} = 29\frac{2}{6}$ or $29\frac{1}{3}$

$14\frac{5}{9} - 7\frac{6}{9} = 6\frac{8}{9}$

$10 \times \frac{7}{8} = \frac{70}{8}$ or $\frac{35}{4}$

$13\frac{7}{11} + 9\frac{9}{11} = 23\frac{5}{11}$

$4 \times \frac{9}{12} = \frac{36}{12}$ or $\frac{3}{1}$

$19\frac{3}{8} - 6\frac{5}{8} = 12\frac{6}{8}$ or $12\frac{3}{4}$

$18\frac{5}{7} + 23\frac{4}{7} = 42\frac{2}{7}$

PAGE 151

6 cups

$7\frac{3}{4}$ cups

$\frac{3}{4}$ of a cup

$1\frac{2}{3}$ cups

PAGE 152

$\frac{6}{10}$ $\frac{3}{10}$ $\frac{8}{10}$

$\frac{70}{100}$ $\frac{55}{100}$ $\frac{37}{100}$

PAGE 153

$\frac{3}{10} = 0.3$ $\frac{8}{10} = 0.8$ $\frac{96}{100} = 0.96$

$\frac{4}{10} = 0.4$ $\frac{25}{100} = 0.25$ $\frac{6}{10} = 0.6$

$\frac{48}{100} = 0.48$ $\frac{9}{100} = 0.09$

PAGE 154

Fraction	Decimal
$\frac{59}{100}$	0.59
$\frac{23}{100}$	0.23
$\frac{15}{100}$	0.15
$\frac{9}{10}$	0.9
$\frac{7}{100}$	0.07
$\frac{81}{100}$	0.81
$\frac{2}{10}$	0.2
$\frac{3}{100}$	0.03

PAGE 155

$\frac{3}{4} = \frac{75}{100} = 0.75$ $\frac{12}{25} = \frac{48}{100} = 0.48$

$\frac{3}{5} = \frac{6}{10} = 0.6$ $\frac{35}{50} = \frac{70}{100} = 0.70$

$\frac{1}{4} = \frac{25}{100} = 0.25$ $\frac{1}{2} = \frac{5}{10} = 0.5$

$\frac{18}{20} = \frac{90}{100} = 0.90$

PAGE 156

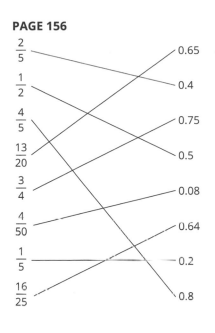

$\frac{2}{5}$ — 0.65

$\frac{1}{2}$ — 0.4

$\frac{4}{5}$ — 0.75

$\frac{13}{20}$ — 0.5

$\frac{3}{4}$ — 0.08

$\frac{4}{50}$ — 0.64

$\frac{1}{5}$ — 0.2

$\frac{16}{25}$ — 0.8

PAGE 157

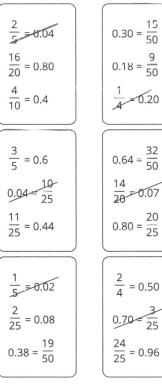

$\frac{2}{5}$ = 0.04

$\frac{16}{20}$ = 0.80

$\frac{4}{10}$ = 0.4

$0.30 = \frac{15}{50}$

$0.18 = \frac{9}{50}$

$\frac{1}{4} = 0.20$

$\frac{3}{5}$ = 0.6

$0.04 = \frac{10}{25}$

$\frac{11}{25}$ = 0.44

$0.64 = \frac{32}{50}$

$\frac{14}{20} = 0.07$

$0.80 = \frac{20}{25}$

$\frac{1}{5} = 0.02$

$\frac{2}{25}$ = 0.08

$0.38 = \frac{19}{50}$

$\frac{2}{4}$ = 0.50

$0.70 = \frac{3}{25}$

$\frac{24}{25}$ = 0.96

PAGE 158

0.24 < 0.4   0.8 > 0.08
0.43 < 0.5   0.9 < 0.91
0.60 = 0.6   0.34 > 0.2
0.1 > 0.07   0.8 > 0.75

PAGE 159

0.32 > 0.30   0.75 > 0.72   0.59 < 0.8
0.39 < 0.48   0.12 > 0.1   0.30 = 0.3
0.1 > 0.09   0.65 < 0.7   0.6 > 0.06
2.1 < 2.17   4.8 = 4.80

PAGE 160

1.03
0.5
1.68
2.3
1.1

PAGE 161

0.25
4.09
0.8

PAGE 162

feet
pounds
gallons

PAGE 163

inches
tons
cups
miles
ounces
cups
yards
ounces
gallons

PAGE 164

Gallons	Pints
1	8
2	16
3	24

Yards	Feet
1	3
2	6
3	9

Pounds	Ounces
1	16
2	32
3	48

Tons	Pounds
1	2,000
2	4,000
3	6,000

PAGE 165

154 yd. = 462 ft.   5 gal. = 20 qt.
57 pt. = 114 c.   429 qt. = 858 pt.
4,500 yd. = 13,500 ft. 17 lb. = 272 oz.
36 lb. = 576 oz.   4 tons = 8,000 lb.

PAGE 166

10 pints
32 quarts
10,000 pounds
224 ounces
21,120 feet

PAGE 167

58 pints = 29 quarts   36 feet = 12 yards
60 quarts = 15 gallons   72 inches = 6 feet

PAGE 168

45 hours = 2,700 minutes
9 weeks = 63 days
7 minutes = 420 seconds
12 years = 144 months
3 years = 156 weeks
59 weeks = 413 days
27 days = 648 hours
24 hours = 1,440 minutes

PAGE 169

millimeters
kilograms
milliliters

PAGE 170

centimeters
grams
liters
kilometers
kilograms
liters
millimeters
grams
milliliters

PAGE 171

Liters	Milliliters
1	1,000
2	2,000
3	3,000
4	4,000
5	5,000

Centimeters	Millimeters
1	10
2	20
3	30
4	40
5	50

Meters	Centimeters
1	100
2	200
3	300
4	400
5	500

Kilograms	Grams
1	1,000
2	2,000
3	3,000
4	4,000
5	5,000

PAGE 172

49 L = 49,000 mL

36 kg = 36,000 g

72 m = 7,200 cm

200 cm = 2,000 mm

18 cm = 180 mm

5 km = 5,000 m

45 L = 45,000 mL

582 kg = 582,000 g

620 L = 620,000 mL

PAGE 173

140 millimeters

180,000 grams

300 centimeters

23,000 meters

25,000 milliliters

PAGE 174

428 in.

663 cm

500 yd.

$2\frac{2}{8}$ or $2\frac{1}{4}$ in.

$2\frac{4}{5}$ m

PAGE 175

11 in.

58 mm

18 feet

379 centimeters

19 cm

79 ft.

PAGE 176

88 square yd.

105 square ft.

729 square cm

117 square in.

216 square m

$3\frac{1}{5}$ square in.

PAGE 177

12 in.

23 mi.

32 ft.

15 m

26 cm

27 yd.

PAGE 178

45 square yards

160 meters

21 feet

108 inches

Yes. She will need only 768 square feet of wallpaper.

PAGE 179

95 square ft.

144 square ft.

450 square in.

PAGE 180

400 square cm

464 square m

1,272 square cm

PAGE 181

acute   obtuse   right

obtuse   acute

PAGE 182

right   acute   right

obtuse   acute

PAGE 183

scalene   isosceles   equilateral

isosceles   scalene

PAGE 184

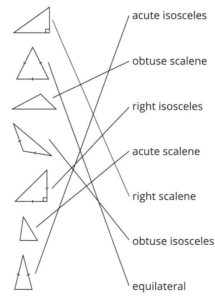

acute isosceles

obtuse scalene

right isosceles

acute scalene

right scalene

obtuse isosceles

equilateral

PAGE 185

perpendicular   parallel

neither   neither

parallel   perpendicular

PAGE 186

Answers may vary. Some possible answers are shown below.

Main Street and Ash Street are perpendicular to each other.

Beech Avenue and Birch Street are parallel to Willow Road.

Maple Street and Greene Avenue are not parallel or perpendicular to each other.

Oak Street and Main Street are perpendicular to Ash Street.

PAGE 187

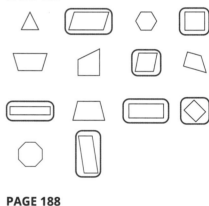

PAGE 188

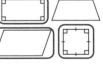

PAGE 189

PAGE 190

45°   130°

60°   155°

PAGE 191

75°	20°
115°	35°
175°	140°

PAGE 192

180°

90°

PAGE 193

right

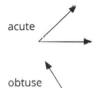

acute

obtuse

PAGE 194

75°	110°
63°	159°
124°	38°

PAGE 195

18°	62°
69°	120°
43°	64°
67°	

PAGE 196

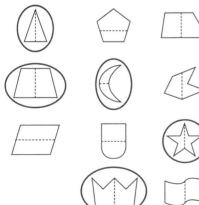

PAGE 197

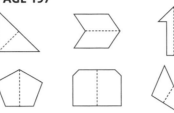

PAGE 198

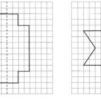

PAGE 199

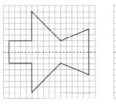

PAGE 200

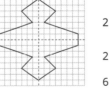
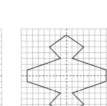
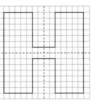
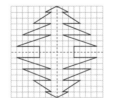
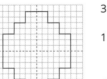
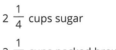

PAGE 201

Erica's score is 8.7.

Kaitlyn's score is 8.5.

Amelia's score is 9.25.

Charlotte's score is 7.95.

Molly's score is 9.8.

Answers may vary. A possible answer is shown below.

8.2

PAGE 202

$2,421

PAGE 203

406 child passes

373 adult passes

$31

$11

$8,940

PAGE 204

$3 \frac{2}{4}$ or $3 \frac{1}{2}$ teaspoons

$1 \frac{2}{4}$ or $1 \frac{1}{2}$ cups

PAGE 205

$3 \frac{3}{4}$ cups

Yes, because $\frac{2}{4}$ is equal to $\frac{1}{2}$.

$2 \frac{1}{4}$ cups sugar

$2 \frac{1}{4}$ cups packed brown sugar

6 eggs

3 teaspoons baking soda

$1 \frac{1}{2}$ teaspoons salt

$\frac{3}{4}$ cup butter, softened

3 packages cream cheese

PAGE 206

147 square feet

$294

PAGE 207

63 square feet

$112

429 square feet

$2,145

639 square feet